Discover ...

Topics for Advanced Learners

Series editor: Klaus Hinz

D1723900

Aspects of the English Language

Student's Book

Edited by Ralf Weskamp

Best.-Nr. 40045 2

Verlag Ferdinand Schöningh

Gedruckt auf umweltfreund-
lichem, chlorfrei gebleichtem
Papier.

Alle deutschsprachigen Teile
dieses Werks folgen der refor-
mierten Rechtschreibung und
Zeichensetzung.

Umschlag: Veronika Wypior
Illustrationen: Christiane Zay

© 1997 Ferdinand Schöningh, Paderborn
(Verlag Ferdinand Schöningh, Jühenplatz 1, 33098 Paderborn)

Printed in Germany. Gesamtherstellung: Ferdinand Schöningh,
Paderborn.

Druck 5 4 3 2 1   Jahr 01 00 99 98 97

ISBN 3-506-40045-2

Contents

Abbreviations and Pronunciation Table   4
Getting Started   5

Chapter 1   "Whose English is it, anyway?" –
World Englishes   7

• Larry E. Smith: A Chauvinistic Language   8
• Loreto Todd: Pidgins and Creoles 11
• William Shakespeare: The Red Plague Rid You for
  Learning Me Your Language 14
• Raja Rao: Kanthapura 16
• Kim Campbell: American English – Colonial
  Substandard or Prestige World Language? 18

Chapter 2   "We've never talked to each other" –
Language and Communication 24

• Stephan Gramley, Kurt-Michael Pätzold:
  Spoken Discourse 25
• Harold Pinter: Are They Nice? 27
• David Cook: It Was Called the Bungalow 30

Chapter 3   "Let your women keep silent in the churches" –
Language and Gender 34

• Suzanne Romaine: Men versus Women 35
• Carol Shields: Good Morning, Dr Maloney 37
• Joan Swann: It Is Male Speakers Who Talk More 39

Chapter 4   Invasions and Cultural Revolution –
The Making of English 42

• Trevor A. Harley: The Origin of Language 43
• Robert McCrum, William Cran, Robert MacNeil:
  The Spread of RP 46
• Cal McCrystal: Proud Celts Reverse Tide of History . . . 49

Chapter 5   "A sense of what a dialogue among Neanderthals
might have been" – Language and Modern Media 53

• Michael Heim: Language Threatened 54
• Philip Elmer-Dewitt: Bards of the Internet 57

Abbreviations
and Pronunciation Table

Short forms and labels

AmE	American English
BrE	British English
c.	circa, about
Ind.	Indian English
inf.	informal
jmd.	*jemand*
p.	page/pages
pl.	plural form
s.o.	someone
s.th.	something
sl.	slang

English phonetic symbols and signs

Vowels

Short		Long		Diphthongs	
ɪ	pit	iː	bean	eɪ	bay
e	pet	ɑː	barn	aɪ	buy
æ	pat	ɔː	born	ɔɪ	boy
ʌ	putt	uː	boon	əʊ	no
ɒ	pot	ɜː	burn	aʊ	now
ʊ	put			ɪə	peer
ə	another			eə	pair
				ʊə	poor

Consonants

g	**g**ame	ŋ	lo**ng**	ʃ	**sh**ip
tʃ	**ch**ain	θ	**th**in	ʒ	mea**s**ure
dʒ	**J**ane	ð	**th**en	j	**y**es

p,b,t,d,k,m,n,l,r,f,v,s,z,h,w have their usual English sound values.

Stress accent: [ˈ...] the following syllable carries primary stress, [ˌ...] the following syllable carries secondary stress.

Getting Started

This book is intended for you as students of the German *Gymnasiale Oberstufe,* but may also be useful if you enrol in introductory courses in English linguistics at university.

Its aim is not only to present information about various aspects of the English language, but also to encourage you to explore and experience creatively how language works, to what extent language use may become problematic, how language is constantly changing, etc.

Furthermore, this book should not be seen as a formal coursebook to be followed from start to finish. It is rather a resource of aspects of the English language which can be studied independently from each other. This also implies that you have a choice concerning the tasks and that you can concentrate on parts which you and your teacher find especially interesting and rewarding.

Skimming involves reading very quickly through a text or book to get an overall idea of its content. This technique helps you for example to find out whether a text or book is of interest to you.

Now, have a closer look at the table of contents and skim through the book to find out what you are going to deal with. You can also discuss the extent to which this book differs from other books you have worked through before.

◀ **A first task**

The following tasks should help you to get an idea of the role English already plays in your lives.

Work with a partner. Choose one of the following assignments:

◀ **Finding out about English around you**

1. Go for a walk in your town. Make a note of everything that contains English expressions. Then write these expressions down on a poster to present it in class.

2. Record TV-advertisements or collect ads from newspapers. Make a collage of English expressions used and show it in class.

3. Read an issue of a German quality magazine or newspaper. Write down sentences in which English words are used. Present your findings to the whole class.

Chapter 1: "Whose English is it, anyway?" – World Englishes

Start here

English as a world language ➤ It can be said that English is the most widely taught, read, and spoken language in the world. However, it seems strange at first sight that the language of a relatively small country could have reached such a status.

In the following chapter you will see that two factors made this possible: the colonial power Great Britian had attained by the end of the 19th century and the economic power of the United States in the 20th century.

Thinking about pros and cons ➤ Before you go on reading have a look at the pictures and think over positive and negative aspects of English as a world language.

A Chauvinistic Language
Larry E. Smith

Make a guess

Predicting what information you may find in a text helps you to focus more effectively on its main ideas. The text below deals with English as an international language.
Consider the title and the illustration and formulate three questions you might expect to be answered. Compare your questions with those of your neighbours; then read the text.

*Do you agree with this?
What about other countries?*

We are at present witnessing a rapid increase in the use of English as a language of wider communication. It is the language of air-traffic controllers at international airports all over the world. It is the language used most frequently for international mail and at international conferences. It is the principal language of 5 international commerce and international aid. The geographical spread of English indicates its rising importance. Often it is claimed that it has reached such importance because of its total number of fluent users (both native and non-native) scattered all over the globe. Sometimes it is said to be so important because 10 it was the language of the industrial revolution and remains the language of science and technology. No doubt two reasons for the high frequency of its use are (1) the power and influence of native English speaking countries, and (2) the fact that much world communication either originates from a native English 15 speaking audience or is directed to such an audience. However, I believe a more important reason for the ever increasing high frequency of its use is that non-native speakers are using it more and more often with other non-native speakers in international settings. More and more countries are making English their *lin-* 20 *gua franca* to communicate with the rest of the world – not just the native English speaking world. This is happening at the same time that English is being used *less* frequently as a nation-

Countries where English has an official status

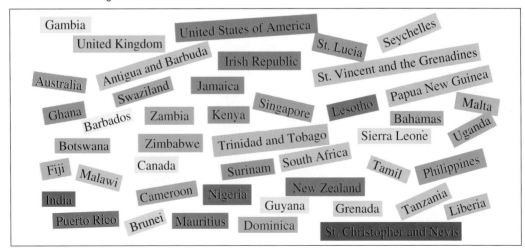

al language because of the desire to reaffirm indigenous cultur-
25 al identities. The message seems to be, "English is not one of
our national languages, but it is our international language. And
English as an international language is not the same as English
as a second or foreign language." (Smith)

When any language becomes international in character, it
30 cannot be bound to any one culture. A Thai doesn't need to
sound like an American in order to use English well with a Fil-
ipino at an ASEAN meeting. A Japanese doesn't need an appre-
ciation of a British lifestyle in order to use English in his business dealings with a Malaysian. The Chinese do not need a
35 background in western literature in order to use English effectively as a language for publications of worldwide distribution.
The political leaders of France and Germany use English in private political discussions but this doesn't mean that they take on
the political attitudes of Americans. It is clear that in these situ-
40 ations there is no attempt for the user to be like a native speaker
of English. English is used to express the speaker's business
policy, government position, or political conviction. It is the
means of expression of the speaker's culture, and *not* an imitation of the culture of Great Britain, the United States or any oth-
45 er native English speaking country.

English, when used as an international language, is not
owned by its native speakers, and native and non-native speakers everywhere must become aware of the widespread shift in
attitudes and assumptions about the language. This shift from a
50 native-speaker dominated to *any*-speaker oriented attitude toward English is expressed in a statement made by T.T.B. Koh,
Singapore's representative to the United Nations, "… when one
is abroad, in a bus or train or aeroplane and when one overhears
someone speaking, one can immediately say this is someone
55 from Malaysia or Singapore. And I should hope that when I'm
speaking abroad my countrymen will have no problem recog-
nizing that I am a Singaporean." Of equal importance in expressing this shift in attitude is a statement by Randolph Quirk
that "notions such as English is the Englishman's gift and the
60 language remains fundamentally 'ours', etc. are parochial and
naïve" and that "they do not even remotely correspond to linguistic realities and they can do nothing but harm to the cause of
human relationships and international harmony".

International organizations, like the East-West Center, must
65 not only accept this international position for English but must
promote it and ensure that their staff and programmes are not
chauvinistic toward non-native users of English. This doesn't
mean "anything goes". Each of us must continue to be concerned with what is appropriate, acceptable and intelligible.
70 The most basic concern is for intelligibility. If a person doesn't
speak clearly enough to be understood, his message is lost. It
should be emphasized here however that the responsibility for
effective communication is shared by both the speaker and the
listener. In a conversation, it is not the sole responsibility of the
75 speaker to make himself understood. The listener must make an
effort to understand. It is fortunate that most speakers are able

to reaffirm to state again
indigenous [ɪnˈdɪdʒɪnəs]
originally from the country in
which it is found
≺ What may be the
differences?

≺ To what extent might the
knowledge of Western literature
help a Chinese?

≺ Would you mind if your
accent gave you away when
you travelled (for example) to
England?
notion an opinion or belief

intelligible [ɪnˈtelɪdʒəbl] something able to be understood
≺ What do you associate with
these terms?
to emphasize to say that s.th. is
very important

to attain *erreichen*
mutual ['mju:tʃʋəl] here: common

to attain mutual intelligibility after only a brief exposure to a pronunciation different from their own.

The second concern is for grammatical acceptability. It is often easy to understand a person's meaning from what is said even when that person isn't using grammatical sentences. If we hear a person say, "I miss too much my mother," there is little doubt about the meaning but there is some doubt about the person's English education. Strevens has pointed out that standard English can be spoken with any accent and the use of international English doesn't lower this standard.

negotiator representative
down-home (AmE) related to the values of people living in the countryside
deficit *Mangel*
negotiation discussion

What was Strauss's fault? ➤

sophistication *Kultiviertheit*

emphasis stress

The third concern is for appropriateness. One can be easily understood and speak in grammatical sentences and still use English inappropriately. Robert Strauss, formerly chief foreign trade negotiator, is known for his down-home, friendly style. While working on the deficit trade negotiations with Japan, *Time* magazine reports that as the talks were on the verge of breaking down, Strauss slapped the Japanese Minister on the back and laughing said, "You know what? You're crazy as hell!" That the negotiations did not collaps on the stop is probably due more to the Japanese Minister's sophistication than to Strauss' rich humour. To say that linguistic chauvinism cannot be tolerated in situations where English is used as an international language does not mean that less emphasis will be given to these three concerns: intelligibility, grammatical acceptability, and social appropriateness.

Activities

Going into detail ➤

Discuss in groups whether your questions have been answered and what new information you have gathered from the text.
Make a list of the main ideas. If you use an overhead transparency you can easily present your list to the whole class.

"If you ask me ..." ➤

In class, talk about your personal motives for and aims of learning English. Compare your views with the author's ideas of using a foreign language.

Project – English speaking countries ➤

Try to find the countries shown in the illustration in an atlas. Then get a roll of wallpaper, pencils, crayon, water-colours, etc. and draw your own world map of English speaking countries. This can be a collaborative activity for the whole class.
In groups, choose one of these countries which interests you most and find out as much about it as possible. Write down the main points on the wallpaper for everybody to read.

Pidgins and Creoles   Loreto Todd

Sometimes people mock or imitate immigrants who use language in a slightly different way. Gastarbeiter German is a typical example of such a language called a pidgin.
In class, discuss how Gastarbeiter German differs from the German native people speak. Perhaps you can also interview immigrants in your city and make a list of examples to show where their use of German differs from your own use. Then read the following text to find out more about this phenomenon.

◄ **Gastarbeiter German – A language in its own right?**

   Pidgins and creoles have been given both popular and scholarly attention. Popularly, they are thought to be inferior, haphazard, broken, bastardized versions of older, longer established languages. In academic circles, expecially in recent
5 years, attempts have been made to remove the stigma so frequently attached to them, by pointing out that there is no such thing as a primitive or inferior language. Some languages, it is true, may be more fully adapted to a technologically advanced society but all languages are capable of being modified to suit
10 changing conditions. Yet, while scholars have increasingly come to recognize the importance of pidgin and creole lan-

inferior second-rate
haphazard careless
bastardized *verfälscht*
stigma *Schandmal*

◄ What languages may the author have in mind?
to be capable of to be able to

The widespread nature of the pidgin/creole phenomenon (Not all pidgins and creoles are listed.)

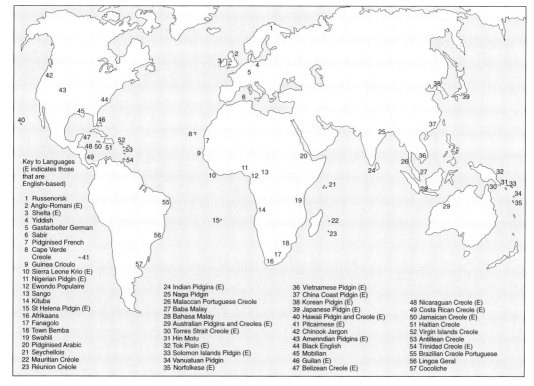

Key to Languages
(E indicates those that are English-based)

1 Russenorsk
2 Anglo-Romani (E)
3 Shelta (E)
4 Yiddish
5 Gastarbeiter German
6 Sabir
7 Pidginised French
8 Cape Verde Creole   ≈ 41
9 Guinea Crioulo
10 Sierra Leone Krio (E)
11 Nigerian Pidgin (E)
12 Ewondo Populaire
13 Sango
14 Kituba
15 St Helena Pidgin (E)
16 Afrikaans
17 Fanagolo
18 Town Bemba
19 Swahili
20 Pidginised Arabic
21 Seychellois
22 Mauritian Créole
23 Réunion Créole

24 Indian Pidgins (E)
25 Naga Pidgin
26 Malaccan Portuguese Creole
27 Baba Malay
28 Bahasa Malay
29 Australian Pidgins and Creoles (E)
30 Torres Strait Creole (E)
31 Hin Motu
32 Tok Pisin (E)
33 Solomon Islands Pidgin (E)
34 Vanuatuan Pidgin
35 Norfolkese (E)

36 Vietnamese Pidgin (E)
37 China Coast Pidgin (E)
38 Korean Pidgin (E)
39 Japanese Pidgin (E)
40 Hawaii Pidgin and Creole (E)
41 Pitcairnese (E)
42 Chinook Jargon
43 Amenndian Pidgins (E)
44 Black English
45 Mobilian
46 Guilan (E)
47 Belizean Creole (E)

48 Nicaraguan Creole (E)
49 Costa Rican Creole (E)
50 Jamaican Creole (E)
51 Haitian Creole
52 Virgin Islands Creole
53 Antillean Creole
54 Trinidad Creole (E)
55 Brazilian Creole Portuguese
56 Lingoa Geral
57 Cocoliche

guages, there has been considerable debate, and disagreement, among them as to the precise meaning to be attached to the terms. The following definitions would, however, be widely accepted as a reasonable compromise. [15]

A *pidgin* is a marginal language which arises to fulfil certain restricted communication needs among people who have no common language. In the initial stages of contact the communication is often limited to transactions where a detailed exchange of ideas is not required and where a small vocabulary, drawn al- [20] most exclusively from one language, suffices. The syntactic

structure of the pidgin is less complex and less flexible than the structures of the languages which were in contact, and though many pidgin features clearly reflect usages in the contact languages, others are unique to the pidgin. A comparison of con- [25] temporary pidgin Englishes, such as, for example, Tok Pisin (Talk Pidgin) in Papua New Guinea (PNG) and Kamtok (Cameroon Talk), the English-based pidgin of Cameroon, with English shows that the pidgins have discarded many of the

inessential features of the standard variety, as two brief illustra- [30] tions should clarify. All natural languages have some degree of redundancy. In many European languages, for example, plural-

ity is marked in the article, the adjective and the noun, as well as, occasionally, by a numeral. In *'les deux grands journaux'* there are, in the written form, four overt markers of plurality, [35] three in the spoken form. English is, in this respect, less redundant than French, but in the comparable phrase 'the *two* big newpaper*s*' plurality is marked by both the numeral and the noun ending. Tok Pisin (the pidgin English of PNG) and Cameroon pidgin are less redundant still, marking plurality by [40]

the numeral only, *tupela bikpela pepa* and *di tu big pepa*. The second example of discarding grammatical inessentials is illustrated in Table 1. English has less verbal inflection than French but both pidgins have an invariable verb form.

Table 1

French	English	Tok Pisin		Kamtok	
je vais	I go	*mi*		*a*	
tu vas	you go	*yu*		*yu*	
il/elle va	he/she/it goes	*em*		*i*	
nous allons	we go	*yumi* *mipela*	*go*	*wi*	*go*
vous allez		*yupela*		*wuna*	
ils/elles vont	they go	*ol*		*dem*	

A *creole* arises when a pidgin becomes the mother tongue of a speech community. The simple structure that characterized the pidgin is carried over into the creole but since a creole, as a mother tongue, must be capable of expressing the whole range

of human experience, the lexicon is expanded and frequently a more elaborate syntactic system evolves.

Mek Four   John Agard

Who seh West Indian creole
is not a language of love?
Well I tell you …

When me and she eye
5 mek four
negative vibration
walk out de door

when me and she eye
mek four
10 tenderness was a guest
that didn't need invitation

when me and she eye
mek four
the world was neither
15 more or less
but a moment of rightness

we tongue locked
in a syntax of yes

mek four meet

Activities

Work together in groups and find out whether you understand the text. The following tasks may help you.

◀ **Understanding the text**

1. Draw a mind-map of the characteristics of pidgin languages:

```
        ...        ...
          \       /
   ... ─( pidgin languages )─ ...
          /       \
        ...        ...
```

2. Discuss how pidgins and creoles differ from each other.

3. Describe how a pidgin can turn into a creole.

The origin of a pidgin language is usually due to colonization (for some basic information see page 15). In class, have a brainstorming session to come up with what you already know about the topic.

◀ **Getting some information about colonization**

Then, in groups, take England as an example and find out more about colonization. You may want to use the town or school library, your history book, encyclopaedias and CD-ROMs as resource materials.

Organize your findings and write an essay. You can then either read it to the whole class or exchange it with another group. Discuss if other people have included ideas which are new to you.

The Red Plague Rid You for Learning Me Your Language

William Shakespeare

The following extract is taken from William Shakespeare's (1564–1616) romantic drama *The Tempest* (c. 1611), perhaps his last complete play. It is the story of the duke Prospero, who – banished by his brother – was cast upon a lonely island, where he has been living with his daughter Miranda for the last twelve years. The native inhabitant of the island is Caliban. The location may be the Bermudas, which were discovered in 1515 and first colonized by the British in 1684.

Before you read the text, discuss the effects of colonization on the peoples of the colonized areas.

Observe Caliban's and Prospero's attitudes towards each other.

unwholesome unhealthy, unpleasant
fen *Sumpfland*
ye (old-fashioned) you, when you are talking to more than one person
to blister *mit Blasen bedecken*
thou (old-fashioned) you, when you are talking to only one person

What has happened in the process of Prospero's reign?

cramps *Krämpfe*
thy (old-fashioned) your, when you are talking to only one person
urchin here: *Igel*
thee (old-fashioned) used like thou, but as the object of a verb or preposition
brine-pit *Salzbrunnen*

toad *Kröte*

to sty here: *einsperren*

stripes here: beating

Enter CALIBAN.

CALIBAN: As wicked dew as e'er my mother brush'd
    With raven's feather from unwholesome fen
    Drop on you both! a south-west blow on ye
    And blister you all o'er!
PROSPERO: For this, be sure, to-night thou shalt have cramps,   5
    Side-stitches that shall pen thy breath up; urchins
    Shall, for that vast of night that they may work,
    All exercise on thee; thou shalt be pinch'd
    As thick as honeycomb, each pinch more stinging
    Than bees that made 'em.   10
CALIBAN: I must eat my dinner.
    This island's mine, by Sycorax my mother,
    Which thou tak'st from me. When thou cam'st first,
    Thou strok'st me, and made much of me; wouldst give me.
    Water with berries in't; and teach me how   15
    To name the bigger light, and how the less,
    That burn by day and night: and then I lov'd thee,
    And show'd thee all the qualities o' th'isle,
    The fresh springs, brine-pits, barren-place and fertile:
    Curs'd be I that did so! All the charms   20
    Of Sycorax, toads, beetles, bats, light on you!
    For I am all the subjects that you have,
    Which first was mine own King: and here you sty me
    In this hard rock, whiles you do keep from me
    The rest o' th' island.   25
PROSPERO: Thou most lying slave,
    Whom stripes may move, not kindness! I have us'd thee,
    Filth as thou art, with human care; and lodg'd thee
    In mine own cell, till thou didst seek to violate
    The honour of my child.   30
CALIBAN: O ho, O ho! would't had been done!
    Thou didst prevent me; I had peopled else
    This isle with Calibans.

MIRANDA: Abhorred slave,
35 Which any print of goodness wilt not take,
Being capable of all ill! I pitied thee,
Took pains to make thee speak, taught thee each hour
One thing or other: when thou didst not, savage,
Know thine own meaning, but wouldst gabble like
40 A thing most brutish, I endow'd thy purposes
With words that made them known. But thy vile race,
Though thou didst learn, had that in't which good natures
Could not abide to be with; therefore wast thou
Deservedly confin'd into this rock,
45 Who hadst deserv'd more than a prison.
CALIBAN: You taught me language; and my profit on't
Is, I know how to curse. The red plague rid you
For learning me your language!

abhorred hateful

◄ What does Miranda mean when she says "to make you speak"?
to gabble to speak very quickly
brutish like an animal
I endow'd ... I taught you the use of language and enabled you to say what was going on in your mind
to abide to hate

plague *Pest*
to rid to destroy

Colonialism is the policy of a state to extend control over weaker peoples and areas. Modern European colonialism dates from the 15th century. From 1415 to about 1800, Western Europe led by Spain and Portugal expanded in the East Indies and the Americas; from 1800 to World War II the British Empire became the largest colonial network around the world and expanded to Asia, Africa, and the Pacific. Since World War II colonization has been discussed more and more controversially and this has led to a rapid decolonization.

Activities

In groups, list Caliban's and Prospero's/Miranda's main arguments during their conversation.

◄ **Caliban's and Prospero's arguments**

Prospero/Miranda	Caliban	Comment
	– this is my island	Caliban thinks that Prospero has taken away his island
...		

Can you make Caliban's language physical? Work together in pairs. One reads Caliban's monologue (lines 11–25), the other mimes a gesture for each of Caliban's thoughts.
Talk about your experiences during this activity with the whole class and discuss what feelings Caliban might have had in this situation.

◄ **Playreading**

Caliban's sentence "the red plague rid you for learning me your language" is an important statement in the context of colonization.
In class, discuss this statement. What does the learning of Prospero's language, i. e. English, mean for Caliban?

◄ **The play in the context of colonization**

Kanthapura Raja Rao

While reading >

Post-colonial literatures (also New Literatures in English, World Literature in English, or Commonwealth Literature): A term used to cover the writings by authors who were born in countries other than Great Britain and the United States and who share the experience or the effects of colonization.

Raja Rao was born in Mysore, India, in 1908. There he has been living most of his life except for some time he spent studying in France and lecturing in the USA. *Kanthapura*, published in 1938, is Rao's first novel and describes a non-violent revolt of an Indian village against a British plantation owner.

While reading, observe how Rao discusses the problems of writing such a novel in English and how this is illustrated by his use of a special Indian vocabulary.

Foreword

My publishers have asked me to say a word of explanation.

How are Indian villages different from German ones?
Rama hero of *Ramayana,* one of the the two great Sanskrit epics
pipal-tree (Ind.) large fig-tree
Sita heroine of *Ramayana*

to mingle to mix
repertory here: all her stories
annals chronicles

to convey to express

to maltreat to treat badly

There is no village in India, however mean, that has not a rich sthala-purana, or legendary history, of its town. Some god or godlike hero has passed by the village – Rama might have rested under this pipal-tree, Sita might have dried her clothes, after 5 her bath, on this yellow stone, or the Mahatma himself, on one of his many pilgrimages through the country, might have slept in this hut, the low one, by the village gate. In this way the past mingles with the present, and the gods mingle with men to make the repertory of your grandmother always bright. One 10 such story from the contemporary annals of my village I have tried to tell.

The telling has not been easy. One has to convey in a language that is not one's own the spirit that is one's own. One has to convey the various shades and omissions of a certain thought- 15 movement that looks maltreated in an alien language. I use the word 'alien', yet English is not really an alien language to us. It is the language of our intellectual make-up – like Sanskrit or Persian was before – but not of our emotional make-up. We are all instinctively bilingual, many of us writing in our own lan- 20 guage and in English. We cannot write like the English. We should not. We cannot write only as Indians. We have grown to look at the large world as part of us. Our method of expression therefore has to be a dialect which will some day prove to be as distinctive and colourful as the Irish or the American. Time 25 alone will justify it.

What do life and language have in common?
to infuse to fill with s.th.

to tumble to move with quick movements, perhaps often falling
interminable never-ending

After language the next problem is that of style. The tempo of Indian life must be infused into our English expression, even as the tempo of American or Irish life has gone into the making of theirs. We, in India, think quickly, we talk quickly, and when we 30 move we move quickly. There must be something in the sun of India that makes us rush und tumble and run on. And our paths are paths interminable. The Mahabharatha has 214,778 verses and the Ramayana 48,000. Puranas there are endless and innu-

Rajasthan: a small village in India

merable. We have neither punctuation nor the treacherous 'ats'
and 'ons' to bother us – we tell one interminable tale. Episode
follows episode, and when our thoughts stop our breath stops,
and we move on to another thought. This was and still is the ordinary style of our story-telling. I have tried to follow it myself
in this story:

It may have been told of an evening, when as the dusk falls
and through the sudden quiet, lights leap up in house after
house, and stretching her bedding on the veranda, a grandmother might have told you, newcomer, the sad tale of her village.

An extract from the novel

Till now I've spoken of the Brahmin quarter. Our village had
a Pariah quarter too, a Potters' quarter, a Weavers' quarter, and
a Sudra quarter. How many huts had we there? I do not know.
There may have been ninety or a hundred – though a hundred
may be the right number. Of course, you wouldn't expect me to
go to the Pariah quarter, but I have seen from the streetcorner
Beadle Timmayya's hut. It was in the middle, so – let me see –
if there were four on this side and about six, seven, eight that
side, that makes some fifteen or twenty huts in all. Pock-marked
Sidda had a real *thothi* house, with a big veranda and a large
roof, and there must have been a big granary somewhere inside,
for he owned as much land as Patwari Nanjundia or Shopkeep-
er Subba Chetty, though he hadn't half Kanthapura as Bhatta
had. But lately, Sidda's wife went mad, you know, and he took
her to Poona and he spent much money on her. Bhatta, of
course, profited by the occasion and added a few acres more to
his own domain. Clever fellow this Bhatta! One day he was sure
to become the Zamindar of the whole village – though we all
knew him walking about the streets with only a loin-cloth about
him.

Brahmin (Ind.) member of the highest of the four Hindu castes, usually priests

⋎ Why doesn't the author simply translate the Indian words?
Pariah (Ind.) member of a low class or no caste at all
Sudra (Ind.) fourth and lowest Hindu caste, usually labourers, fishermen, and servants
pock-marked *pockennarbig*
thothi (Ind.) inner courtyard
granary *Kornkammer*

Zamindar (Ind.) landlord

Activities

Writing in English ▷ In groups, make a list of the reasons Rao gives why it is so difficult for him to write in English. Then discuss why he and other post-colonial writers keep using English. Write down your findings and compare them with those of another group.

Reading the story ▷ Find out what Rao says about story-telling. Then, in groups, try to read the extract from the novel as it may have been told by the grandmother from whose point of view the novel is written.

Rehearse your reading in front of the class. Then discuss how well Rao has succeeded in transmitting the Indian way of thinking through the English language.

Language = culture – ▷ The central idea of the so-called **Sapir-Whorf hypothesis** is
The Sapir-Whorf that our language determines the way in which we perceive
hypothesis the world. Eskimo, for example, has four words for snow, some forms of Arabic have a large number of words for "camel", because these things are important in their respective worlds. The American Indian language Hopi has only one word for insect, pilot, and plane, since the idea of human beings flying in planes is alien to their view of the world.

Discuss the Sapir-Whorf hypothesis taking *Kanthapura* and your own experiences into account. For a start try to find out the English word for German *Teig* and the German word for English *chemist*.

American English – Colonial Substandard or Prestige World Language? Kim Campbell

Different kinds of ▷ The following text deals with British and American English.
English Before you read it consult your monolingual dictionary and find out about differences between the two varieties.

Dialects or varieties are different in grammar and vocabulary, whereas **accents** differ only in pronunciation. So American English, British English or creoles are varieties of English.

You can also watch BBC World, CNN, or NBC Superchannel, which are provided by most cable firms, and talk about differences between the Englishes of the speakers.

Like many Russians, Ilya Bezouglyi learned English the way his teachers preferred: British style.

But after being laughed at in Canada for using the word "chaps," and after a year of graduate study in the United States,
5 Mr. Bezouglyi says that he and his English are "pretty much Americanized."

The "Americanization" of English is happening around the world today, from Africa to Britain itself. American English is seeping into the nooks and crannies of English everywhere
10 thanks to education, business, Hollywood, and the Internet.

Although British English – which many countries consider to be the "real thing" – is widely taught around the world, what those learners use in their private lives is more influenced by the US.
15 As a result, "American English is spreading faster than British English," says Braj Kachru, a linguist in India and a founder and co-editor of the journal "World Englishes."

In television broadcasts alone, the United States controlled 75 percent of the world's programming as recently as 1993, beam-
20 ing "Sesame Street" to Lagos, Nigeria, for example.

Americans also outnumber Britons: People are more likely to encounter one of the 260 million Yanks than one of the 55 million Brits. "It's more practical to speak and understand American English these days," says Bezouglyi, who adds there are
25 more Americans than Britons in Russia today.

Ⓨ What influences *your* English more: American or British English?

every nook and cranny all parts of

◄ For more on the Internet consult the last chapter of this book.

to encounter to meet with

New York City

Note the historical reasons ⋎
for the spread of American and
British English.
to recede to move gradually
away

What may be the differences ➤
between a native, a foreign,
and a second language?

Why do you think American ⋎
English may be more pres-
tigious than British English?

clout power, influence

notorious *berüchtigt*

badge sign of membership
How does the use of English ⋎
differ around the world?

curriculum (pl. curricula)
Lehrplan
to blossom *blühen*

The spread of American English began in the decades after World War II. Experts say the simultaneous rise of the US as a military and technological superpower and the receding of the British empire gave many in the world both the desire and option to choose American English. 30

English in general has spread during that time as well. More than 1 billion people are thought to speak it as a native, second, or foreign language. Among the roughly 350 million native English speakers, the American version is spoken by about 70 percent. 35

"There's no question that Britain made English an international language in the 19th century with its empire", says Bill Bryson, an American author of several books on the history of English. "But it's Americans that have been the driving force behind the globalization of English in the 20th century" be- 40 cause of their commercial and cultural clout, he says.

Examples of the influence of American English include:
- Young people in Europe, Asia, and Russia using it in casual conversation – including the notorious US export, "you guys" – even when many of them have been taught British English. 45 "As far as I can see, it's exactly equivalent to wearing Nike baseball caps, or Air Jordan shoes," says Mr. Bryson, who listened to teenagers speak with American accents in the Netherlands recently. "It's a kind of linguistic badge."
- In Brazil, people often ask for courses in "American", rather 50 than English, according to Bernabe Feria, head of curriculum and development for Berlitz International in Princeton, N. J.
- In Nigeria, years of trade with the US – and contact that blossomed in the 1960s with the Peace Corps – have greatly increased the use of American English. It is now spoken along 55 with British English, a leftover of British colonial rule.
- In Cairo, as recently as 1984, some university students received lower grades if they used American spellings instead of British. Since then, there has been an increase in the number of teachers in Egypt trained by Americans. "You can well 60 imagine that nobody gets a red line through their paper for spelling 'center' with an 'er' anymore," says Richard Boyum, the head of English-language teaching activities at the United States Information Agency (USIA).
- In Thailand, the standard in both schools and the English-lan- 65 guage press is British English. But university teachers may speak English with an American accent because they have studied in the USA.
- The British Broadcasting Corporation (BBC), long the promoter of proper British English, now includes Americans in 70 its broadcasts. Its English-language teaching programs feature Americans in broadcasts that go to countries where American English is favored, such as South Korea.

American invasion

75 Britain has not been immune to the spread of American English, either.

More words that were exclusively American are now found in the speech and writing in both countries, says Norman Moss, compiler of an American-British/British-American dictionary
80 called "What's the Difference?" "Once 'guy' and 'campus' were almost unknown in Britain," he says. Today they are widely used.

Britons are also increasingly saying "movie" instead of "film". Computer-related words are more frequently spelled the Ameri-
85 can way: program, without the British addition of "me" on the end, for example. And the American phrase "the bottom line" is encroaching on its British equivalent "at the end of the day."

"We tend to take them [Americanisms] over if they are useful and reject them if they are not," offers Geraldine Kershaw, a se-
90 nior English-language teaching consultant to the British Council, a government-sponsored agency that operates British-English teaching centers worldwide.

Linguists note that the mixing of British and American English in Europe has given rise to a "mid-Atlantic" English, a
95 more neutral language that is less identifiable with either country.

In some European countries, both kinds of English are now accepted and taught. Some learners prefer American English because they believe it has fewer regional accents and dialects
100 than British English does, experts say, and therefore is easier to understand and to use.

Still, the USIA – which advises countries on English teaching but does not teach it directly – and its British counterpart, the British Council, argue that the languages are not in competition.
105 "I don't think there is a fierce contest going on between the two kinds of English," says Ms. Kershaw of the British Council. She notes that there are very few differences between the two.

Neither of the agencies "has a budget that could anywhere satisfy the demands that foreign institutions are placing on up-
110 grading English-language expertise," notes the USIA's Mr. Boyum. "What we do in this field is actually mostly cooperate rather than compete."

English as a commodity

But, the question of who is teaching the world to speak Eng-
115 lish is no small matter. The hunger for the language has made English teaching a big business.

"English has become an economic commodity," says Dr. Kachru, who runs the Center for Advanced Study at the University of Illinois in Champaign.
120 Some estimates place the revenues of the worldwide industry at about $10 billion annually. That includes teaching, textbooks, and materials, and money spent by foreign students who choose to attend schools in English-speaking countries as a result of learning the language.

∀ Note the influence of American English on British English.

at the end of the day / the bottom line (inf.) finally

≺ What may be the reasons for the use of "mid-Atlantic" English?

fierce wild, erbittert,heftig

budget a financial plan
to upgrade to improve
expertise [ˌekspɜːˈtiːz] know-how

commodity s.th. sold for money

∀ How can you sell a language?

estimate Schätzung
revenue [ˈrevənjuː] income

The dollar amount will likely get much bigger if predictions 125 by the British Council that more than 1 billion people will be learning English by 2000 prove true. Markets that are expected to contribute to the rise include Russia and China. China alone is estimated already to have between 200 million and 400 million people who speak some form of English. 130

Currently, much of the English taught in Europe, India, and parts of Asia and Africa is British or British-influenced. American English is favored in Latin America, Japan, and South Korea.

Does this also apply to you? ➤

But linguists note that often those learning the language just 135 want English – they don't care what kind. English is often studied by people whose primary purpose is not to speak to Americans or Britons, says Dr. Feria of Berlitz. They need to speak with other non-native speakers, using English as a common language, experts say. 140

Many cultures also increasingly communicate in their own forms of English – Indian English, for example. And some countries may reject either American or British English if speaking it is considered undesirable for political reasons.

Nevertheless, English teaching generates more than $1.1 bil- 145 lion annually for Britian. The British Council pulls in about $237 million of that from its global, self-supporting English

to launch [lɔ:ntʃ] to begin

teaching and related activities. Last year, it launched its English 2000 program. One of its aims is to attract more foreign students to Britain through promotion of British English and cul- 150 ture worldwide.

Australia is also in the game, adding an estimated $415 million annually to its economy from teaching English. It, too, has become more aggressive recently, establishing English-teaching centers in Asia as a way to attract foreign students to Aus- 155 tralian universities.

Although the US government discontinued its involvement in direct English teaching in the 1970s, the US still attracts 450,000 students and scholars to American schools each year.

dissemination spread

They, in turn, become a powerful dissemination vehicle (in ad- 160 dition to bringing more than $7 billion annually to the American economy).

"Each one of them obviously learns American English, and in fact some of them go back and become teachers of it abroad," says John Loiello, associate director for cultural and education 165 affairs at the USIA.

In addition, it is thought that those who learn one kind of Eng-

to immerse *eintauchen*

lish or another, especially when they learn it while immersed in the culture of a country, are more likely to buy the goods of that country in the future. 170

Muscovite Bezougly is a case in point. He reads Newsweek magazine and frequents a newly opened American bookstore in

What do you do to improve ➤ your English?

Russia. He says he chooses to read American publications because he better understands "what they're writing about and their English." 175

As English continues to spread, some experts say, a form of it could become the common language of the world. But multilingualism is also on the rise, suggesting that English may not be the only language to prevail.

180   David Crystal, a linguist from Wales and author of the Cambridge Encyclopedia of the English Language, says that the way English is changing now, if it does become the global language, "it's going to be American-English-dominated, I have no doubt."

to prevail to continue to exist

Activities

Work together with a partner. Construct a multiple choice test containing 8 items with 4 choices each. Here is an example:

The driving force behind the spread of English in the 20th century
○ was the television industry
○ were the British
○ was Berlitz International
○ was McDonald's

Then pass on your test to another pair to fill in the answers. Discuss the answers with this pair.

◄ **Developing a multiple choice test**

Discuss in class which variety of English you would prefer to speak: British English, American English, or mid-Atlantic English. Give reasons for your choice.

◄ **Which variety?**

Discuss in groups to what extent the spread of American English also means a spread of American culture. First, reflect upon what "American culture" is and what traces of it you can find in your own country.
Then write a short report on your findings which you can read to the whole class for discussion.

◄ **Writing a report**

Steps in writing a report:
(1) Gather [further] material
(2) Collect as many ideas as possible
(3) Organize your ideas into groups so that you have a clear structure
(4) Write a first version of your report
(5) Discuss it with a fellow student
(6) Revise your report
(7) Write a final version

Chapter 2: "We've never talked to each other" –

Language and Communication

Start here

Contemplating communication ➤ Keep a diary in which you write down notes of longer conversations you have with other people. Structure your entries as follows:

- With whom?
- About what?
- Who talked more?
- What was the general mood or feeling during your talk?

In class, compare your diary with those of other students. Then talk about similarities and differences.

Spoken Discourse
Stephan Gramley, Kurt-Michael Pätzold

The following text focuses on talk between two or more people, i.e. linguistically speaking "spoken discourse". Before you read the text, discuss in class what may be the differences between spoken and written discourse.

◀ **Spoken and written communication**

Conversation is a social activity in which language plays a decisive, if not exclusive, role. Non-verbal ways of communication such as gestures, body language and eye contact can underscore or contradict what is said and show whether someone
5 likes people and is attentive to what they say or, indeed, it can signal whether someone is willing to talk to them in the first place. While non-verbal aspects of speech are of great importance, the focus of this chapter will be largely on the verbal aspects of conversation.

decisive [dɪˈsaɪsɪv] *ausschlaggebend*
to underscore to underline

10 Many of the rules that make for smooth social intercourse in general also apply to talk between two or more people. Among these are, above all, consideration for others. In most cases, people are assumed to be honest, reasonable, truthful and trustworthy individuals. If life in society is to be tolerable, not to say
15 profitable, then people must try to accept others the way they are or at least the way they choose to present themselves, avoid offending them, and help them to preserve face. For conversations this means, for example, that each S should accept the other's topics, let them have their say and give their opinions a fair
20 hearing without challenging or interrupting them too often. Hs should make Ss feel at their ease, show them that they are prepared to give them their full attention, are interested in what they think, agree with them as far and as often as possible, and generally avoid saying unpleasant things to them. These are as-
25 pects of what has been called the **hearer-support maxim.** If Ss do not receive feedback, support and encouragement, they cannot be expected to do the same the other way round. Conversely, supporting the H implies not forcing one's own wishes and desires on others (too often and too blatantly), on the assump-
30 tion hat Hs will support Ss in their turn. Some writers have noticed a decrease in social reciprocity, i.e. in the ability to give and take, and put this down to economic and social insecurity in modern individualistic societies, which causes many middle-class people to promote themselves constantly and thus come to
35 be 'preoccupied with themselves and unattentive to their companions' (Pin and Turndor).
A further aspect of polite behaviour is that one should repay compliments or other verbal behaviour by which people show that they are interested in us. This is particularly easy to observe
40 in what is called **phatic communion.** Awareness of the H also shows in the choice of when to talk and when to be silent. Silence causes embarrassment because it usually indicates a conversational breakdown. People who can only talk and not listen (conversational bullies or 'steamrollers'), or who can only lis-

consideration here: thoughtfulness

S speaker

to challenge *herausfordern*
H hearer

blatantly *aufdringlich*

reciprocity *Gegenseitigkeit*

preoccupied to think a lot about s.th.

phatic communion language which does not convey meaning but has a purely social function (e.g. "How do you do?")
steamroller (inf.) here: s.o. who forces you to accept her/his ideas

to shun to reject

tacit unspoken

ten and not talk, make others feel uncomfortable and are in dan- 45 ger of being shunned. How to begin a conversation, what topics to introduce and what particular aspects to mention – all these are matters of conventions, which may differ from society to society. In many English-speaking countries, for instance, it is usual to keep away in everyday conversation from areas of po- 50 tential conflict and to avoid introducing too many new ideas or going too deeply beneath the surface. Native speakers learn these conventions as they grow up in their societies as a matter of course, but foreigners do not necessarily share these tacit assumptions. Over and above a grammatical (i.e. syntactic, pho- 55 netic, phonological, lexical and semantic) knowledge of the language in question, non-native speakers have therefore to acquire what has been called a **communicative competence** in the foreign culture, memorably summed up by Hymes: 'competence as to when to speak, when not, and as to what to talk 60 about with whom, when, where, in what manner'.

The **grammar** of language consists of three different levels:
- **Phonology** concerns itself with the sound of language
- **Morphology** deals with the combination of sounds that carry single meanings (e.g. "un-" in front of an adjective expresses a negative meaning)
- **Syntax** is the way in which units of meaning are combined into words, phrases, and sentences

Furthermore, semantics refers to the study of meaning, lexis to the study of words; phonetics examines the production of sounds, whereas phonology deals with sounds and how they produce differences in meaning.

Activities

The hearer-support maxim

One of the central themes of the text is the so-called "hearer-support maxim", which also plays an important role in this chapter.
Together with a partner, collect all aspects of the hearer-support maxim given in the text on an overhead transparency. Present your results to the whole class.
Then discuss what may happen if aspects of the hearer-support maxim are violated. Try to give examples from your own experiences.

Gathering experiences >

Try to comply consciously with all aspects of the hearer-support maxim for one day. Write down your experiences and report them to your class.

Gramley and Pätzold also write about "communicative competence" in a foreign language. In class, discuss what they mean by this term. Take the information box on "How to say sorry" into account as well.

◀ **Communicative competence**

How to say sorry

Most non-native speakers think that to say "very sorry" or "really sorry" is very much the same. However, native speakers make a distinction: "really" expresses deeper regret, apology, and concern. For example, if you have scalded someone with coffee in a cafeteria it may be rude to say "very sorry" instead of "really sorry".

Are They Nice? Harold Pinter

Harold Pinter, who was born in London in 1930, is one of the most challenging and original playwrights in Britain. In his plays he is primarily concerned with individuals in their personal relationships. These relationships are set in an absurd, even hostile world, in which the characters are unable to control their fates. His most notable plays include *The Birthday Party* (1957), from which the following extract is taken, *The Dumb Waiter* (1957), and *The Caretaker* (1960).

Work in pairs. Imagine you are having breakfast together. Write down what you would talk about. Then write a short sketch and act it out in front of the class.

◀ **Writing a sketch**

> *The living-room of a house in a seaside town. A door leading to the hall down left. Back door and small window up left. Kitchen hatch, centre back. Kitchen door up right. Table and chairs, centre.*
> 5 PETEY *enters from the door on the left with a paper and sits at the table. He begins to read.* MEG'*s voice comes through the kitchen hatch.*

MEG. Is that you, Petey?

Pause.

10 Petey, is that you?

Pause.

Petey?

PETEY. What?
MEG. Is that you?
15 PETEY. Yes, it's me.

hatch *Durchreiche*

ⅴ Observe how often there is a pause. What may be the function of the pauses?

MEG. What? *(Her face appears at the hatch.)* Are you back?
PETEY. Yes.
MEG. I've got your cornflakes ready. *(She disappears and reappears.)* Here's your cornflakes.

to prop up *aufrichten*

He rises and takes the plate from her, sits at the table, props 20
up the paper and begins to eat. MEG *enters by the kitchen
door.*

> **Stage directions** are notes that tell the actors how to speak and act in a play. They also say what the characters and the stage should look like and where and when the action takes place.
> Furthermore, stage directions help the reader who cannot see the play performed on stage to get a vivid idea of what is going on.

    Are they nice?
PETEY. Very nice.
MEG. I thought they'd be nice. *(She sits at the table.)* You got 25
    your paper?
PETEY. Yes.
MEG. Is it good?
PETEY. Not bad.
MEG. What does it say?   30
PETEY. Nothing much.
MEG. You read me out some nice bits yesterday.
PETEY. Yes, well, I haven't finished this one yet.
MEG. Will you tell me when you come to something good?
PETEY: Yes.   35

    Pause.

to stack to form a neat pile

MEG. Have you been working hard this morning?
PETEY. No. Just stacked a few of the old chairs. Cleaned up a bit.
MEG. Is it nice out?
PETEY. Very nice.   40

    Pause.

MEG. Is Stanley up yet?
PETEY. I don't know. Is he?
MEG. I don't know. I haven't seen him down yet.
PETEY. Well then, he can't be up.   45
MEG. Haven't you seen him down?
PETEY. I've only just come in.
MEG. He must be still asleep.

    *She looks round the room, stands, goes to the sideboard and
    takes a pair of socks from a drawer, collects wool and a nee-* 50
    dle und goes back to the table.

    What time did you go out this morning, Petey?
PETEY. Same time as usual.
MEG. Was is dark?
PETEY. No, is was light.   55
MEG *(beginning to darn)*. But sometimes you go out in the
    morning and it's dark.
PETEY. That's in the winter.
MEG. Oh, in winter.
PETEY. Yes, it gets light later in winter.   60
MEG. Oh.

What have Meg and Petey ⋀
been talking about so far?

    Pause.

What are you reading?

PETEY. Someone's just had a baby.
65 MEG. Oh, they haven't! Who?
PETEY. Some girl.
MEG. Who, Petey, who?
PETEY. I don't think you'd know her.
MEG. What's her name?
70 PETEY. Lady Mary Splatt.
MEG. I don't know her.
PETEY. No.
MEG. What is it?
PETEY (*studying the paper*). Er – a girl.
75 MEG. Not a boy?
PETEY. No.
MEG. Oh, what a shame. I'd be sorry. I'd much rather have a
little boy.
PETEY. A little girl's all right.
80 MEG. I'd much rather have a little boy.

Pause.

PETEY. I've finished my cornflakes.
MEG. Were they nice?
PETEY. Very nice.
85 MEG. I've got something else for you.
PETEY. Good.

Activities

In groups, discuss your first impression of Meg and Petey. You can also speculate on their age, their outward appearance, their movements during their dialogue, the tones of voice they use.

Then have a closer look at the dialogue. Discuss how the author achieves the effect of giving you this special impression of Meg and Petey. Report your findings to the whole class.

Try to find out if the hearer-support maxim (cf. "Spoken Discourse" by Stephan Gramley and Kurt-Michael Pätzold) is violated. Make a list of examples from the text. Compare your examples with those of another group.

◄ **The characters and how they talk**

Imagine you are a marriage counsellor who has been consulted by Meg and Petey about their marital problems. You are now writing a report in which you explain how the relationship of the couple has developed through the years. You also include some advice which you may want to give them on how to solve their problems.

Then either exchange your report with another student for discussion, read it to the whole class or roleplay a meeting with Meg and Petey in which you advise them on the basis of your report.

◄ **Writing a report**

Discussing other people's opinions ➤

Identify the key ideas of the following quotations. Can you agree with them?

"His characters commonly say very little, or even nothing, when they mean very much. Often, too, they camouflage their real meaning, substituting a sort of code for direct statement. Arguments about whether it is correct to say 'light the kettle' or that wasps 'bite' are the outer and visible signs of inner and deeper discord […]."

Benedict Nightingale, *An Introduction to Fifty Modern British Plays*, London: Pan, 1982, p. 345.

to camouflage to cover
to substitute to replace

discord disharmony

"One of the reasons that she [Meg] sounds like a silly old woman is that her vocabulary is still that of a bride enjoying providing breakfast for her husband and looking forward to the baby that she hopes will be a boy. Her unquenchable folly, and Petey's resigned acceptance of her good intentions, have a quality of heroism which survives even the laughter of the audience."

Nigel Alexander, "Past, Present and Pinter", *Das Englische Drama nach 1945*, ed. Klaus Peter Steiger, Darmstadt: Wissenschaftliche Buchgesellschaft, 1983, p. 297.

unquenchable *unaufhörlich*
resigned to accept without complaining

"Pinter's characters are often abject, stupid, vile, aggressive: but they are always intelligent enough in their capacity as conscientious and persistent liars, whether lying to others or to themselves […]. They are perverted in their actions and speech: hence human."

Guido Almansi, "Harold Pinter's Idiom of Lies", *Contemporary English Drama*, ed. C.W.E. Bigsby, London: Arnold, 1981, p. 80.

abject *erbärmlich, unterwürfig*
vile [vaɪl] ghastly, *abscheulich*
persistent constant

It Was Called the Bungalow
David Cook

A good social worker ➤

The following scene is taken from David Cook's novel *Second Best* (1991), the story of a single man in his thirties who decides to adopt a ten year old boy. It describes a meeting between James, the boy, and his care worker.
Before you read the scene, discuss in pairs what makes a good care worker. Write down your ideas and compare them with those of another pair.

It was called the Bungalow. You went there with your 'special person', your Key Worker, to draw, paint, make models, play with toys, bake cakes, or simply to lie on the floor staring up at the ceiling. You were supposed to say anything which came into your head; that was the point of it. The Bungalow was sup- 5 posed to be like home, like a real home, except that although there was a kitchen and a bedroom with a single bed, nobody lived there and all the rooms were very small and filled mostly with kids' things.

10 You were supposed to talk freely to your special person, to express yourself; you had an hour to do that. Away from other children and other staff, you were free to concentrate on yourself. 'Free expression' it was sometimes called, but James knew that what things were sometimes called and what they were of-15 ten differed. An important element of these hour-long sessions would be your Life Story Book. You didn't have to work on it. It could be left unopened if you chose, but then leaving it unopened would be commented on and you would be asked why. 'Didn't you feel up to thinking about the past, James?' That was 20 why you went to the Bungalow, to find out about what had happened to you and why, so that everyone could begin to feel better about it.

'Do you want to talk about your Life Story Book?' Bernard was James's special person at the moment. They knew better 25 now than to assign him a woman. Bernard never needed quick replies to his questions and that was in his favour. He was about twenty-seven, with bleary sad eyes which made him look permanently hung-over, and still wore what used to be called tank tops and are now exclusive to Oxfam shops.

30 'Why?'

'Just thought that now your're taking this adoption business seriously, we should do some work on your past.'

'Who said I was taking it seriously?'

'I do have a small bit of news. If you're interested.'

35 Whenever the word 'news' was mentioned to James, another word came into his mind. This word was 'parole' and was really a word of Jimmy's. It was a word confined to Jimmy's mind only, and would never be uttered by James, who yawned, stretched himself, turned to face Bernie the Tank Top, and, in 40 order to indicate the amount of interest he felt, placed his elbow on the floor and leaned his chin on the palm of his hand.

'Don't start frothing at the mouth, will you? I did say a small piece of news.'

'Bit. You said "bit". It goes in a horse's mouth.'

45 'Is that a fact? Well now, this information did in a sense come straight from the horse's gob, so shall we open the book at the "My Third Year" page, then?'

It was like one of those children's programmes on the television, with rituals and set rules. At each of these sessions it must 50 always be James who opened the book, because it was his book about his life. The fiction was that it was James himself who wanted to re-examine what had happened to him. Otherwise the session would do no lasting good.

James got to his feet wearily, crossed the room to where the 55 Life Story Book was and fingered the corners of the pages to count them so that when he opened the book it would be at the relevant page and no other. There would be no unnecessary trips down memory lane, no sudden flashes of anger or fear, no catatonic starings at out-of-focus snapshots, no jumping from 60 James to Jimmy and back again. There would be no loss of con-

A Why doesn't the care worker simply use his office?

⋎ Observe how "free expression" is done in the following

to assign *jmd. zuweisen*

bleary [ˈblɪərɪ] tired
tank top *Pullunder*
Oxfam Oxford Committee for Famine Relief

parole *bedingter Straferlass*
⋎ What do the two names signify?

froth at the mouth *Schaum vor dem Mund haben*

gob (inf.) mouth

catatonic state in which you cannot think, speak, or move

trol, just a weary, uninterested ten-year-old playing out the Bungalow game with a camphor-scented tank top standing too close behind him.

'Look at the page, and tell me in your own time what you re- 65
member.'

'Tell me the news first.'

'Then will you talk to me about this page?'

'Thought you didn't approve of bribery.'

'God, you're a bloody difficult sod to help, do you know that?' 70

James said, 'That's more like "free expression". You're getting the hang of it now. And yes I do know, as a matter of fact.'

'This page. You looking at it?'

'I'm looking.'

'Heavens for small mercies.' 75

'Well?'

'Well, we think we might know the name of your maternal grandparents. That's your born-to mother's parents.'

'I do know what "maternal" means, strange as it may seem. Can I close the book now?' 80

'No. You haven't said anything about that page.'

'What's to say? You could write their name down if you like and I could add some question marks after it. That suit you?'

'Read me what's written on the page.'

'You're joking!' James slammed the book shut and moved to 85 the other side of the room, picking up a toy car from the floor as he did so.

Whenever they moved him, wherever he went, there was one question he would always be asked sooner or later. Sometimes the question would be asked in the form of a statement of dis- 90 belief. 'But you must have a photograph of her.' Enquiries would follow, letters would be written, phone calls made, and he would listen to the calls or be shown the letters. 'We have a very distressed young boy here, who has no photograph of his born-to mother. I wonder if you can help at all?' On and on it 95 went. Those of whom the enquiries were made never could help, because there was no photograph of James's born-to mother, whose name and whereabouts were unknown to any of the authorities.

'You're nowhere near ready to start a new life with a new fam- 100
ily, are you?'

'Who's going to stop me?'

'You are. You're going to stop yourself. No one is going to agree to your moving in with a new father when they realize you haven't said your goodbyes to the old one. I'm supposed to help 105 you get in touch with deep-rooted feelings, help you take them out, look at them, and pack them away again. I have to know what stage you're at, or at the very least give a fair impression of knowing. I have to represent you and to tell them honestly if I think you're ready. I know all this seems to you like an exer- 110 cise designed to upset you, but believe me, it's for your own good.'

'Gobbledygook!'

---

bribery to offer s.o. money in order to persuade
sod (sl.) bastard, swine

to get the hang of to begin to understand

maternal motherly

Why is a photo of such ➤ importance?

distressed unhappy, suffering

What does this word ➤ indicate?

Activities

Discuss in class the extent to which your ideas of a good care worker are confirmed or contradicted by Bernard.

 Discussion

Imagine you are James. Discuss in class how you would feel during the conversation.
Then work together with a partner. Make a table in which you list what Bernard and Jimmy are saying and how communication is failing here. For example, Bernard's question "Do you want to talk about your Life Story Book?" is not honest, because they are going to talk about the book regardless. (Cf. information box)

Analysing the communication

In groups, rewrite the scene so that communication between James and Bernard becomes more natural. Present your results to your class.

Rewriting the scene

Communication can be described as the sharing of meaning in order to develop relationships. To assess a good relationship you can ask yourself the following questions: are you able to
• talk about feelings, weaknesses, desires, or fears?
• show your emotions (e.g. cry and laugh)?
• accept the way things are?
• be honest and open?
• listen to the other?
• talk about your communication (e.g. why you don't understand the other any more, or why you hurt the other one's feelings)?

Chapter 3: "Let your women keep silent in the churches" – Language and Gender

Start here

Analysing texts ➤ Bring magazines, comics, books, video recorded TV advertisements, etc. with you. Work together in groups. Investigate how girls and boys and women and men are represented. Make a collage of the examples you found most interesting and present it to the whole class.

Then study the illustration below and talk about differences between the two sexes. Do they correspond to your findings?

Women are better at...

Speed of perception You have to determine quickly which of the houses are alike. Women are better at this simple test than men

Visual memory You have to memorise a group of objects so you can spot what has changed – here the box has gone missing. Women win again

ladder, lock, lunatic, lift, lice, lounge, lichen, loft, lycra, larder, lamp, lent, lager, letter, loser, liar

Verbal skills You have to come up with nouns beginning with the same letter. Women produce more examples

Men are better at...

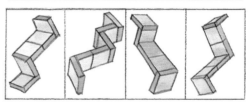

Mental projection of movement Here you have to work out which of the three objects on the right is the same object as the one on the left. Men are better at this

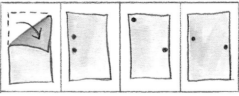

Spatial perception You have to work out which of the three sheets on the right matches the other one. This tests a similar ability to the one tested above

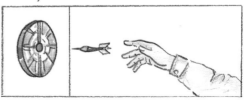

Targeted movement Men are much better at catching and throwing objects at a distant target

Men versus Women

Suzanne Romaine

According to the biblical account of God's creation of the two sexes, Eve is formed later by God's taking a rib from Adam. This image also seems to apply to language. Think of occupational terms: "author" for example was first and became "authoress". Even female names are often derived from the male version, e.g. Pauline or Henrietta.

In groups, find more examples of sexism in language. Then discuss in class whether this shows that men indeed are the superior sex.

◀ **The second sex?**

Sexism in language can be demonstrated with many different kinds of evidence. Words for women have negative connotations, even where the corresponding male terms designate the same state or condition for men. Thus, *spinster* and *bache-*
5 *lor* both designate unmarried adults, but the female term has negative overtones to it. Such a distinction reflects the importance of society's expectations about marriage, and more importantly, about marriageable age. The Pope is also technically a bachelor, but by convention, he is not referred to as one since
10 he is obliged not to marry. A spinster is also unmarried but she is more than that: she is beyond the expected marrying age and therefore seen as rejected and undesirable. These are cultural stereotypes.
   The bias is far-reaching and applies even to our associations
15 of *man* versus *woman*. No insult is implied if you call a woman an 'old man', but to call a man an 'old woman' is a decided insult. Where similar terms exist, such as *mother* or *father,* their meanings are different. To say that a woman *mothered* her children is to draw attention to her nurturing role, but to say that a
20 man *fathered* a child is to refer only to his biological role in conception. The notion of mothering can be applied to other people and children other than one's own, whereas fathering cannot. More recently, the term *surrogate mother* has been used to refer to a woman in her biological role as mother. As I was writing
25 this book, such a surrogate mother was the first woman to give birth to her own grandchildren. Now there are many kinds of mothers, e.g. *biological mother, surrogate mother, unwed mother, single mother, birth mother, working mother,* and even *natural mother.* The fact that these notions vary from our cultural
30 stereotype of housewife-mother is signalled linguistically by the use of special terms to refer to them. We make inferences from such terms and use them in our thinking about men and women. There is no term *working father* because it is redundant. Likewise, we do not normally talk of *single* or *unwed fa-*
35 *thers* because there is no stigma attached to this status for men.
   Because the word *woman* does not share equal status with *man,* terms referring to women have undergone pejoration. If we examine pairs of gender-marked terms such as *lord/lady,*

evidence *Beweis*
connotation association, undertone
to designate *bezeichnen*

◀ What German examples come to mind?

to oblige here: *verpflichten*
spinster rather old, unmarried woman

◀ How would you define "stereotype"?
bias prejudice

to nurture *aufziehen*
conception *Empfängnis*
notion idea, concept

◀ This is Romaine's central statement. Do you agree?
inference ['ɪnfərəns] conclusion, assumption
redundant not needed
stigma *Makel*

pejoration [ˌpiːdʒəˈreɪʃən] *Herabsetzung*

wizard a man with magic powers

to devalue to lessen

derogatory having a very low opinion
brothel *Bordell*

discrepancy difference
hussy a woman of shocking or immoral behaviour

biddy (sl.) elderly woman
tart a woman considered attractive, but in a vulgar way
endearment a loving word

baronet/dame, Sir/Madam, master/mistress, king/queen, wizard (warlock)/witch, etc., we can see how the female terms may start out on an equal footing, but they become devalued over time. *Lord,* for instance, preserves its original meaning, while *lady* is no longer used exclusively for women of high rank. *Baronet* still retains its original meaning, but *dame* is used derogatorily, especially in American usage. *Sir* is still used as a title and a form of respect, while a *madam* is one who runs a brothel. Likewise, *master* has not lost its original meaning, but *mistress* has come to have sexual connotations and no longer refers to the woman who has control over a household. There is a considerable discrepancy between referring to someone as an *old master* as opposed to an *old mistress.* Both *hussy* and *housewife* have their origin in Old English *huswif,* but *hussy* has undergone semantic derogation. *King* has also kept its meaning, while *queen* has developed sexual connotations. *Wizard* has actually undergone semantic amelioration, or upgrading: to call a man a wizard is a compliment, but not so for the woman who is branded (or in medieval times burned) as a witch.

Words like *biddy* and *tart* have changed dramatically since they were first used as terms of endearment. *Tart* meant a small pie or pastry and was later extended to express affection. Then

it was used to refer to a woman who was sexually desirable and to a woman of the street. In general, it seems that English has many more terms to refer to a sexually promiscuous female than to a sexually promiscuous male. According to one count,
65 there are 220 words for such women, while only twenty for men. Some of the more common derogatory terms applied to men, such as *bastard* and *son of a bitch,* actually degrade women in their role as mothers. Because it is men who make the dictionaries and define meanings, they persistently reserve the
70 positive semantic space for themselves and relegate women to a negative one.

promiscuous [prə'mıskjʊəs] having many short sexual relationships

persistently repeatedly
to relegate to make less important

Activities

Work together in groups and add Suzanne Romaine's examples to your list of sexism in language.

◄ **Examples from the text**

Discuss the following points in class:

◄ **Discussion**

1. Romaine says that there are 220 terms to "refer to a sexually promiscous female" but only 20 which refer to such a man. What in your opinion does this statement show?

2. Very often "he" in a text means "he" + "she". Why do you think we don't use "s*he*" = "she" + "he" since "she" contains "he"?

3. Experiments have shown that women feel excluded when they read texts with generic "he". Have the female students in your class had similar experiences? Discuss what can be done to overcome this problem.

Good Morning, Dr Maloney
Carol Shields

Carol Shields was born in Chicago and has lived in Canada since 1957. Though none of her novels was published in Britain until 1990, *Mary Swann* (written 1987) immediately was considered an excellent read. The following extract is the beginning of this novel.

◄ **Female stereotypes**

While reading observe how Shields plays with the stereotype image of women and women's language.

My name is Sarah Maloney and I live alone. Professionally – this is something people like to know these days – I'm a feminist writer and teacher who's having second thoughts about the direction of feminist writing in America. For twenty-five years we've been crying: *My life is my own.* A moving cry, a resounding cry, but what does it *mean*? (Once I knew exactly what freedom meant and now I have no idea. Naturally I resent this loss of knowledge.)

Last night Brownie, who was sharing my bed as he does most Tuesday nights, accused me of having a classic case of burnout, an accusation I resist. Oh, I can be restless and difficult! Some days Virginia Woolf is the only person in the universe I want to talk to; but she's dead, of course, and wouldn't like me anyway. Too flip. And Mary Swann. Also dead. Exceedingly dead.

These moods come and go. Mostly Ms. Maloney is a cheerful woman, ah indeed, indeed! And very busy. Up at seven, a three-kilometre run in Washington Park – see her yupping along in even metric strides – then home to wheat toast and pure orange juice. Next a shower, and then she gets dressed in her beautiful, shameful clothes.

I check myself in the mirror: *Hello there,* waving long, clean, unpolished nails. I'll never require make up. At least not for another ten years. Then I pick up my purse-cum-briefcase, Italian, $300, and sally forth. *Sally forth,* the phrase fills up my mouth like a bubble of foam. I'm attentive to such phrases. Needful of them, I should say.

I don't have a car. Off I go on foot, out into a slice of thick, golden October haze, down Sixty-second to Cottage Grove, swinging my bag from my shoulder to give myself courage. Daylight muggings are common in my neighbourhood, and I make it a point to carry only five dollars, a fake watch, and a dummy set of keys. As I walk along, I keep my Walkman turned up high. No Mozart now, just a little of cushion oft soft rock to help launch the day with hope and maybe protect me from evil. I wear a miraculous broad-brimmed hat. The silky hem of my excellent English raincoat hisses just at knee length. I have wonderful stockings and have learned to match them with whatever I'm wearing.

"Good morning, Dr. Maloney," cries the department secretary when I arrive at the university. "Good morning, Ms. Lundigan," I sing back. This formal greeting is a ritual only. The rest of the time I call her Lois, or Lo, and she calls me Sarah or Sare. She's the age of my mother and has blood-red nails and hair so twirled and compact it looks straight from the wig factory. Her typing is nothing less than magnificent. Clean, sharp, uniform, with margins that *zing.* She hands me the mail and a copy of my revised lecture notes.

Today, in ten minutes, Lord help me, I'll be addressing one hundred students, ninety of them women, on the subject of "Amy Lowell: An American Enigma." At two o' clock, after a quick cheese on pita, I'll conduct my weekly seminar on "Women in Midwestern Fiction." Around me at the table will be

to have second thoughts to have doubts

resounding loud and echoing

to resent to dislike

Why doesn't Sarah just call ➤ Brownie her boyfriend?

to resist to refuse to accept

Consult an encyclopaedia and ➤ find out more about Virginia Woolf.

flip (inf.) *ausgeflippt*

exceedingly very much

Why is Sarah now talking ∀ about herself in the third person?

stride a long step

shameful *beschämend*

to sally forth to go somewhere quickly

mugging robbery

cushion *Kissen, Polster*

to launch to begin

hem *Saum*

Why is the greeting ritual ∀ so important for Sarah?

twirled *gelockt*

Find out more about ➤ Amy Lowell.

enigma [ɪˈnɪgmə] mystery, puzzle

seven bright postgraduate faces, each of them throwing off kilo-
55 watts of womanly brilliance, so that the whole room becomes
charged and expectant and nippy with intelligence.

nippy *spritzig, frech*

> A **stereotype** is a fixed general image or characteristic that
> a lot of people believe in. For example, there is the stereo-
> type of Germans who like law and order. This may be false
> and yet most Germans will be convinced that "Ordnung
> muss sein" and therefore many foreigners believe that Ger-
> mans are very disciplined people.

Activities

Work together in groups. Your task is to create a character
poster of Sarah Maloney. At the centre of the poster fix a re-
presentation of Sarah. This can either be a drawing or a picture from a magazine of a person who you find looks like her.
Around the picture write everything down which can be said
about Sarah.
Present your results to the other students and discuss them
in class.

◄ **Character poster**

> **Irony** is the contrast between
> what is said and what is
> meant. A favourite device of
> irony is hyperbole or exagger-
> ation.

In class, discuss in how far the first-person narrator is described as stereotypically feminine. Also refer to the information box on irony.
What do you think was Carol Shields' (being herself a woman) intention in creating a character like Sarah Maloney?

◄ **Discussion**

It Is Male Speakers Who Talk More Joan Swann

In her book *Girls, Boys, and Language* Joan Swann discusses how girls and boys use language. In the introduction she
writes: "Girls and boys have different experiences of education. Even when they go to the same school, play in the same
playground and take part in the same lessons, they will behave differently, and they will be treated differently by others."
In class, discuss whether you can agree with this statement.
Then read the following extract.

◄ **Girls, boys, and language**

Children need to learn not only how to use appropriate accent
and dialect forms, but also how to make conversation appropri-
ately with others. One of the most pervasive images of female
speakers is that of the talkative sex; women are the gossips and

gossip *Klatschweib*

nag s.o. who complains to you continually

Would you agree with this ➤ sentence?
Reflect on this question ➤ before you go on reading.

prescription *Anordnung, Vorschrift*
to hog to take more than one should
floor here: the right to speak in a debate or discussion

captive hostage, prisoner
to spill the beans to reveal s.th.
mundanely [ˌmʌnˈdeɪnlɪ] banal

collaboratively done by two or more people together

to hold forth to speak for a long time
by virtue of *auf Grund*

What do these findings ⋀ reveal about men and women?

Think about each of these ⋁ points. Do you personally have the same impression?

nags, whereas men are the strong, silent sex. Yet those who have ₅ investigated the amount spoken by female and male speakers tend to find the contrary. Studies have been carried out in a variety of public contexts – 'laboratory' studies, classrooms, meetings, analyses of television chat shows – all with similar results: it is male speakers who talk more. ₁₀

One may wonder, then, why the stereotype of the talkative female persists. One explanation provided by Dale Spender is that there is a double standard in operation; women and girls, Spender argues, are meant to talk very little (hence the various prescriptions reminding them of the virtues of moderation). If ₁₅ they go beyond the limits – even if they talk less than men and boys – they are perceived as hogging the floor.

Amount of talk has been associated with conversational dominance. It is suggested that, in talking more, male speakers are better able to get their points across and have their 'say', – so ₂₀ that they are in control of the conversation and it serves their interests more than women's. But talking more will not always have this effect. Imagine a gangster forcing an unwilling captive to spill the beans or, more mundanely, a person desperately trying to get another to put down the newspaper and pay atten- ₂₅ tion to what they're saying. In neither case does the person doing most of the talking seem 'in control'. To know how to interpret amount of talk, it is necessary to know something about the kind of talk that is being produced.

The amount people talk varies considerably. Carole Edelsky ₃₀ examined talk in informally organized university committee meetings. She identified two types of talk: more formal, 'one person at a time' talk, which she called F1 (for 'Floor 1'); and collaboratively developed talk, in which there was much more overlapping speech, termed F2. Edelsky found that ₃₅

> In F1s, the men held forth, took longer turns though not more of them – dominated the construction of the floor by virtue, at least, of the time they took talking. In F2s, men talked less than they did in F1s and occasionally even less than the women in F2s, a rare finding given the usual one of men as the ₄₀ 'big talkers'.

Edelsky's work suggests that the type of talk engaged in affects how much people speak. But this will be influenced by a variety of other factors, including the context (for example, a meeting or a chat with friends at home), who people are speak- ₄₅ ing to, the purposes of the talk, and how speakers perceive their own role.

Investigations of language in interaction have looked not just at how much people speak, but at how conversations are put together and speaking turns organized. Researchers have identi- ₅₀ fied several conversational features that, in the contexts studied, are used more often by female or male speakers. Examples include the following:
• Male speakers tend to interrupt more than female speakers. In mixed-sex talk, female speakers receive interruptions from ₅₅ male speakers.

- Male speakers use more 'direct speech' than female speakers; for example, they make direct rather than indirect requests.
- Female speakers give more conversational support than male speakers – they use 'minimal responses' such as 'Mmh', 'Yeah' and 'Right' to encourage another speaker to continue and questions that enable another speaker to develop their topic.
- Some studies have suggested that female speakers, more than male speakers, use features that indicate tentativeness, such as 'tag questions' ('That's good, isn't it?'), hedges ('I wonder', 'sort of', 'I guess'), and other expressions that make them sound hesitant or uncertain. Other studies have failed to find evidence to support this. Some research suggests that, rather than being associated directly with female speakers, 'tentative' features are used by speakers of either sex in a relatively powerless position.

tentativeness uncertainty
hedge here: *Schutzfloskel*

Activities

◀ **A true/false test**

Work in pairs. Answer T if you think the statement is true and F if you think the statement is false. Correct any false statements so that they accurately express what is in the text.

(a) According to various studies it is male speakers who talk more. This is in accordance with the common stereotype.

(b) Women are supposed to talk little. So if they talk only a little bit more than usual, they seem to be gossips.

(c) The amount of talk has nothing to do with the kind of talk.

(d) Male speakers interrupt more often than women.

(e) Female speakers more often use "tag questions", thus indicating tentativeness.

(f) Women are better conversationalists.

◀ **Our own experiences**

In class, make a list of Joan Swann's main points and discuss situations where you have observed the same or quite the opposite:

Swann's findings	Our own experiences
– Men interrupt more than women …	– …

What conclusions can you draw from these findings? Will they effect your future behaviour?

◀ **A video project**

Record 15 minutes of an English lesson during which a discussion that involves the whole class takes place.
Then watch the recording and find out whether men and women behaved differently during the discussion.

Chapter 4: Invasions and Cultural Revolution – The Making of English

Start here

Influences on the English language ➤ The title of this chapter is "Invasions and Cultural Revolution: The Making of English". In groups, discuss how invasions and cultural changes may have influenced the development of the English language during the last thousand years. Consult history books or encyclopaedias to get some information about crucial events such as the one illustrated below. Compare your findings with those of other groups.

A detail from the Bayeux Tapestry, a masterpiece of eleventh-century art as well as an important historical document. Here the Battle of Hastings is shown.

The Origin of Language
Trevor A. Harley

Using one or more languages is quite normal for us. But where does language come from? Before you read the following text, speculate on the origin of language.
Then in **three** minutes skim through the text and discuss in class what it is about.

◀ **Make a guess**

Where did language come from? Much about its origin and evolution is unclear. Unlike with the evolution of the hands and the use of tools, there is no fossil record available for study. The capacity for language and symbol manipulation must have
5 arisen as the brain increased in size and complexity between 2 million and 300,000 years ago as *Homo sapiens* became differentiated from other species. There are indications that Broca's area, a region of the brain associated with language, was present in the brains of early hominids as long as two million years ago.
10 The vocal apparatus has become particularly well adapted for making speech sounds in a way that is not true of animals: our teeth are upright, our tongues relatively small and flexible, the larynx (or voice-box) lower in the throat, and the musculature of the lips is more finely developed. The fundamental structures
15 of language appear unchanged over the last 60,000 years.
Language need not and indeed could not have arisen in a vacuum. The social set-up of early man might have helped, but many other animals, particularly primates, have complex social organisations yet did not develop language. Other primates
20 have a rich repertoire of alarm calls, gestures, and other sounds. Some words might have been *onomatopoeic* – that is, they sound like the things to which they refer. For example, "cock-oo" sounds like the call of a bird, "hiss" sounds like the noise a snake makes, and "ouch" sounds like the exclamation we make
25 when there is a sudden pain. The idea that language evolved from mimicry or imitation has been called, tongue in cheek, the "ding-dong", "heave-ho", or "bow-wow" theory. However, such similarities can only be attributed to a very few words, and many words are very different in different languages. Further-
30 more, there is much more to language than using words in isolation. What gives human language its power is the ability to combine words together by use of a *grammar*, and it is the evolution of this that is the most contentious issue.
So murky is the origin of language that it is even an issue
35 whether its grammar arose by Darwinian natural selection. At first sight some strong arguments have been proposed against this: there has not been enough time for something so complex to evolve since the evolution of man diverged from that of other primates; it cannot exist in any intermediate form; and possess-
40 ing a complex grammar confers no obvious selective advantage, so it could not have been selected for. The alternative explanation to evolution by selection is that language arose as a side-effect of the evolution of something else, such as the abili-

◀ A rhetorical question invites the readers to supply an answer.
capacity ability

to become differentiated: to become separate

∀ What parts of your body do you need to speak?

larynx [ˈlærɪŋks] *Kehlkopf*

tongue-in-cheek as a joke, not serious
∀ "However" is a so-called *sentence adjunct* and indicates that another point of view follows. Sentence adjuncts are usally placed at the beginning of a sentence. Can you find more sentence adjuncts, which help to organize the text?
to attribute to say that s.th. has a particular quality
contentious controversial
murky not easy to understand
◀ Charles Robert Darwin (1809–1882) published in 1859 his great work *On the Origins of Species by Means of Natural Selection.*
to diverge to become different

sufficient enough

cognitive related to the process of learning, understanding, knowing

to confer to give

Geoffrey Chaucer (c. 1343–1400), who greatly increased the prestige of English as a literary language, was what might be called a Renaissance man: diplomat, civil servant, a major European literary figure; he knew astronomy, mathematics, alchemy; he made diplomatic trips to France, Spain, and Italy. His masterpiece, *The Canterbury Tales,* is a collection of stories set within a pilgrimage to Canterbury Cathedral and represents a microcosm of 14th-century English society.

ty to use more complex manual gestures, or to use tools, or even just as a by-product of other evolutionary forces such as an in-45 crease in overall brain size. Paget proposed that language evolved in intimate connection with the use of hand gestures, so that vocal gestures developed to expand the available repertoire. Corballis argued that the evolution of language freed the hands from having to make gestures to being able to make tools at the 50 same time. On the other hand, Pinker and Bloom argued that grammar could have arisen by Darwinian natural selection. They argued that there was indeed sufficient time for grammar to evolve, that it evolved to communicate existing cognitive representations, and that the ability to communicate thus con-55 fers a big evolutionary advantage to those that can. To give their example, it obviously makes a big difference to your survival if an area has animals that you can eat, or animals that can eat you. The arguments that a specific language faculty could have arisen through natural selection and evolution are also covered 60 by Pinker. It has been further argued that the evolution of language was related to the evolution of consciousness. As can be seen, this whole topic is very speculative; indeed, as Corballis notes, the Société de Linguistique de Paris banned all debate on the origins of language! And we shall not mention it again, apart 65 from to point out that if it can be shown to have evolved, then some portion of it must be genetically transmitted. This is an important topic to which we shall return.

Although the way in which language evolved may be unclear, it is clear that it has changed. Many languages are related to 70

This extract from Geoffrey Chaucer's *Canterbury Tales* illustrates the use of English at the end of the so-called Middle English period (c. 1066–1500). The translation is by Martin Lehnert.

Whan that Aprill with his shoures soote	Wenn milder Regen, den April uns schenkt,
The droghte of March hath perced to the roote,	Des Märzes Dürre bis zur Wurzel tränkt
And bathed every veyne in swich licour	Und badet jede Ader in dem Saft,
Of which vertu engendred is the flour;	Sodass die Blume sprießt durch solche Kraft;
Whan Zephirus eek with his sweete breeth	Wenn Zephyr selbst mit seinem milden Hauch
Inspired hath in every holt and heeth	In Wald und Feld die zarten Triebe auch
The tendre croppes, and the yonge sonne	Erweckt hat und die Sonne jung durchrann
Hath in the Ram his halve cours yronne,	Des Widders zweite Sternbildhälfte dann,
And smale foweles maken melodye,	Wenn kleine Vögel Melodien singen,
That slepen al the nyght with open ye	Mit offnen Augen ihre Nacht verbringen
(So priketh hem nature in hir corages);	– So stachelt die Natur sie in der Brust –:
Thanne longen folk to goon on pilgrimages,	Dann treibt die Menschen stark die Wallfahrtslust,
And palmeres for to seken straunge strondes,	Und Pilger ziehn zu manchem fremden Strand,
To ferne halwes, kowthe in sondry londes;	Zu Heiligen, berühmt in fernem Land;
And specially from every shires ende	Besonders sieht aus Englands Teilen allen
Of Engelond to Caunterbury they wende,	Man freudig sie nach Canterbury wallen,
The hooly blisful martir for to seke,	Dem segensreichen Märtyrer zum Dank,
That hem hath holpen whan that they were seeke.	Der ihnen half, als sie einst siech und krank.

each other. This relationship is apparent in the similarity of many of the words of some languages (e.g. "mother" in English is "Mutter" in German, "moeder" in Dutch, "mere" in French, "maht" in Russian, and "mata" in Sanskrit). It has been shown 75 by more detailed analyses along these lines that most of the languages of Europe, and parts of west Asia, derive from a common source called proto-European. All the languages that are derived from this common source are therefore called Indo-European. Indo-European has a number of main branches: the Ro- 80 mance (such as French, Italian, and Spanish), the Germanic (such as German, English, and Dutch), and the Indian languages. (There are some exception languages, which are European languages that are not part of the Indo-European family. Finnish and Hungarian are part of the Finno-Ugric family, 85 which is related to Japanese. Basque meanwhile is unrelated to any other language.) Languages change over relatively short time spans: clearly Chaucerian und Elizabethan English are substantially different from today, and even Victorian speakers would sound decidedly odd to us today.

∀ For an example of Chaucerian English see text p. 44; for an example of Elizabethan English see Shakespeare on p. 14–15.
Elizabeth I, Queen of England (1558–1603)
Victoria, Queen of England (1837–1901)
decidedly extremely

Activities

In pairs, try to find answers to the following questions:

1. What are the physical features that show that human beings have a capacity for language?

2. What is the author's opinion on the mimicry theory?

3. Why did the Société de Linguistique de Paris ban all debate on the origins of language?

4. What is said about the relationship between European languages?

◄ **Questions about the text**

Work in pairs again. Draw a diagram of the Indo-European languages mentioned in the text. Present it to the whole class and discuss why so many different languages are spoken in Europe although they all have a common basis, namely Indo-European.

◄ **Indo-European languages**

In the text it is mentioned that animals have not developed language. Yet honey bees, for example, produce a complex dance to show other members of their hive where they can find nectar. Some people also believe that whales and dolphins possess a language.
In class, discuss your opinions on this subject and find out how unique human language really is.

◄ **Animal languages**

The Spread of RP
Robert McCrum, William Cran, Robert MacNeil

In class, discuss what feelings you have when you hear people speaking a dialect.

The following text deals with the introduction of the concept of standard English by the British Broadcasting Corporation (BBC).

The years from the end of the First World War in 1918 to the end of the Second World War in 1945 were the heyday of radio in Britain and the United States, the years of Roosevelt's fireside chats to the American people and of Winston Churchill's wartime broadcasts. The establishment in Britain in 1922 of the 5 first radio broadcasting service, the BBC, was a milestone for the English language. As one of its first executives wrote: "The broadcasting of aural language is an event no less important than the broadcasting of visual language [printing], not only in its influence on human relations, but in its influence upon the 10 destinies of the English language." From the first, the BBC had a global – and in those days imperial – attitude toward the English language. Its motto ran "Nation shall speak peace unto nation", and no one doubted what the tongue should be. The question was: what kind of English?   15

In an era of rapid change, there was, first of all, the question of acceptable vocabulary. New inventions could provoke furious public debate: should *airman* be recognized in favour of *aviator*? A British broadcasting authority would have to make such rulings. Then there were foreign borrowings to cope with. 20 Would a mass radio audience understand *Zeitgeist, Weltanschauung* and *Übermensch*, or should the BBC voice say *timespirit, world-outlook* and *superman*? And what about that old British bugbear, Americanisms? What attitude should the new

25 BBC take towards such coinings as *cocktail, joy-ride, pussy-foot, road-hog* and *sneak-thief*? And, perhaps most sentitive of all, what English accent should the BBC adopt?

The approach to a solution, reached in 1926, was to set up the so-called *Advisory Committee on Spoken English* (ACSE). This
30 high-powered group of experts included the poet Robert Bridges, a northerner who argued unsuccessfully for the adoption of a Northern Standard, the American scholar Logan Pearsall Smith, and the Irishman George Bernard Shaw, but was composed chiefly of RP speakers, men such as the lexicographer
35 C.T. Onions; the scientist Julian Huxley; the art historian Kenneth Clark; and Alistair Cooke, then a young journalist. The Committee's declared task was to arbitrate on the usage and pronunciation of words, English and foreign. Decisions were reached by a simple vote, an arbitrary procedure that, in 1936,
40 for example, sensibly favoured *roundabouts* against *gyratory circuses*, but, less sensibly, proposed *stop-and-goes* instead of *traffic lights*. Arbitrations on usage were probably much less influential for the evolution of a spoken Standard English than judgements about pronunciation. Alistair Cooke remembers
45 how the ACSE settled the pronunciation of "canine":

Shaw brought up the word "canine", and he wanted the recommendation to be "cay-nine"… And somebody said, "Mr Shaw, Mr Chairman, I don't know why you bring this up, of course it's 'ca-nine'." Shaw said, "I always pronounce things
50 the way they are pronounced by people who use the word professionally every day." And he said, "My dentist always says 'caynine'." And he said, "Of course, why do you think at 76 I have all my teeth!"

The first Director General of the BBC, Lord Reith, a Scot,
55 himself believed in a broadcast English that would give no offence, as he recalled in a television interview towards the end of his life:

What I tried to get was a style or quality of English which would not be laughed at in any part of the country. I was as
60 vehemently opposed to what variously has been called the Oxford accent or the south-eastern accent – such as the *the-atah*, the *fahside*.

According to Reith, "the language, the speech and pronunciation … that the announcers were taught to speak … was the
65 very best thing we could do". He was, of course, describing RP. Bridges alone seriously challenged the implicit assumption that RP was the only socially acceptable accent for radio. The establishment of a uniform BBC English was partly designed to promote a sense of impersonality and impartiality. A sober recital,
70 it was felt, would seem more accurate. In the early days, the newsreaders wore dinner jackets and, when nothing newsworthy was deemed to have occurred, they said so – and played classical music instead.

Like many pioneers, Reith was an idealist. His broadcasting
75 corporation reflected his aspirations. First, there was the hope

---

coinings invented phrases

▼ What were the tasks of the ACSE?

to arbitrate to decide what is right
arbitrary *willkürlich*

canine teeth near the front of the mouth

▼ What does this anecdote show?

offence *Kränkung*

to challenge to question
implicit indirect
assumption idea

impartiality neutrality
sober serious, thoughtful
recital performance

to deem to think of s.th. in a particular way

aspiration desire, ambition

pervasive widespread

notion idea, concept

Can there be a "right way" of ➤
speaking a language?

to perpetuate to allow to continue

sustained kept for a long time

What were the BBC's aims Ⓐ
according to Read?

that the BBC would promote English on a global scale. "We cherish the decision", as one pamphlet put it, "that our language will remain as we know it now, the optimistic even seeing in it a future world language." Much more potent, and much more pervasive, was this belief: "It would appear … that the higher a 80 community climbs on the social scale, the greater is the degree of uniformity in speech. Whenever language is spoken, there is present in the minds of the speakers the notion that there is a "right way". Accent was one of the factors that perpetuated social inequality, sustained class barriers, and put the lower class- 85 es at a disadvantage. "You cannot raise social standards without raising speech standards," observed one member of the Committee. Overseas, BBC English – transmitted by eight so-called Empire announcers, and later by the World Service – was intended to unite the colonies, later the Commonwealth. Gradual- 90 ly, the English of the airwaves took over from the English of the imperial Civil Service, a vital means of communication among people without a common language.

Within the British Isles, the spread of RP by the BBC, first on radio, then on television, helped to reinforce what was an al- 95 ready strong connection in many people's minds between education and "Standard English" – usually perceived as the pronunciation found in the public schools, the universities, the professions, the government and the church. The influence of this association was, in its day, enormous, even thought RP was spo- 100 ken by only about 3 per cent of the British population, a tiny fraction of the world's English speaking community.

Activities

Focussing on the text ➤

In pairs, complete the following table

The attitude of the BBC towards the English language	*Global, imperial – everybody should speak the same language, namely English*
Problems of the BBC concerning vocabulary	
The task of the ACSE	
Decision-making in the ACSE	
The BBC's attitude toward accent	
The connection between education and standard English	

Compare your results with those of another pair.

One of the ACSE members said that social standards could not be raised without raising speech standards. Discuss this statement in class.

◁ **Language and social class**

One argument for BBC English is the fear that the more varieties there are the greater is the danger that people will not understand each other any more.
Work in groups. Organize an informal debate in which you argue whether there should be only one standard of English or several dialects. The preceeding chapters may also help you to find a position. Each group should write and develop a speech which is then discussed with the whole class. One student can take the chair. She/he gives the name of the person who should speak next and makes sure that everybody has had the chance to give her/his views. She/he also summarizes the results of the discussion.

◁ **Organizing a debate**

Phrases you can use in debates and discussions:
• What are your views on this?
• Do you agree?
• What's your opinion?
• Could I make a suggestion?
• It seems to me that…
• Do you see what I mean?
• Sorry, could you say that again?

Proud Celts Reverse Tide of History Cal McCrystal

"A man who knows a bit about carpentry will make his table more quickly than the man who does not," says Christine Nuttall. The same applies to reading.
So read only the first and the last paragraphs of the following article, which appeared in the Sunday newspaper *The Observer,* and predict what the text is about.

◁ **The contents of the article**

A sustained resurgence of Celtic languages is giving the lie to those who claimed that the European Union would inevitably produce a homogenised culture throughout the British Isles. Even in divided Northern Ireland, an increasing number of
5 Protestant loyalists are learning Gaelic, turning to the Scottish version of the language for inspiration.
The Celtic revival sweeping Wales, Scotland and both parts of Ireland is remarkable for several reasons. It appears not to be identified with nationalist movements. Its ethos is ultra-modern
10 – it is dominated by youth and encouraged in infancy. Its voice is self-assured, topical and unsentimental. It has shown itself capable of surmounting territorial and religious barriers. Most of all, it is heartily pro-European.
In Scotland the 'huge upsurge' of interest in Gaelic has crea-
15 ted a temporary shortage of teachers. Donald MacSween, chief executive of An Comunn Gaidhealach (the Gaelic Association), says that within 25 years Scotland will have 'well over 100,000 fluent Gaelic speakers', compared with the 60,000 recorded by the 1991 census.

sustained *anhaltend*
resurgence revival, reappearrance
homogenised here: uniform

infancy period when you are a very young child
self-assured self-confident
to surmount to deal successfully with difficulties
upsurge a sudden increase

◁ Why is there a shortage of teachers?
Ⅴ Note other Gaelic words in the text.
census *Volkszählung, Erhebung*

In Wales, about a third of the population now has 'some un- 20 derstanding' of Welsh Gaelic, according to Hugh Jones, who runs the Welsh language S4C television.

Since the station came on air 14 years ago, the proportion of children between the ages of three und 15 who speak Welsh has increased from 18 per cent to 24 per cent. 25

But it is in Ireland – long thought to have given up on what remains, officially, the state language – that the resurgence is most marked. Two weeks ago a new terrestrial television channel, Teilifís na Gaeilge, began transmission, sometimes using subtitles to draw in audiences. Its staff has an average age of 27. 30 It pumps out soap operas, pre-school programmes, news, sports and music in a way that would have been anathema to an older generation of Gaelic defenders.

to draw in to involve

anathema s.th./s.o. you disapprove of or hate strongly

The **Celtic languages** were very important at the beginning of the Christian area. They were found in Gaul, Spain, Great Britain, western Germany und northern Italy. However, because of the Anglo-Saxon conquest of Britain in 449 Celtic has hardly left any traces in the English language. Today it is only found in the remote corners of France and the British Isles.

Gaelic watchers in all three countries – and in Cornwall and Brittany – are maintaining a dialogue, trying out each other's 35 ideas to keep up the momentum of the revival. All are unanimous that the promotion of their minority languages will bring economic benefits as well as new cultural pride. Elen Rhys, director of the Cardiff-based language organisation Acen (Accent), reports: 'Not long ago there were two or three translation 40 agencies in Wales to assist companies and individuals to do business here. Today the number runs into three figures.'

In Ireland, Gaelic had come to be associated with aggressive nationalism and priestly power. In 1904 an education commissioner in British-ruled Ireland wrote to Douglas Hyde, founder 45 of the language-promoting Gaelic League: 'I will use all my

to maintain to continue
momentum *Impuls, Schwung*
to be unanimous to agree upon

to be associated with
gedanklich verbunden sein

influence to ensure that Irish as a spoken language shall die out as quickly as possible.'

He was not entirely successful. When three Irish provinces
50 and a bit of the fourth gained independence from Britain in 1921, the new state made Irish the first language. Twenty-two years later, an influential Dublin literary magazine, the *Bell,* editorialised: 'We treasure Gaelic for one outstanding reason – that… it is the one solitary remnant of *living* tradition that links
55 us back to the centuries behind our breaking.' Having said that, the *Bell* tolled dismally: 'The Gaeltacht [Irish-speaking areas], the language, the Revival, everything that was so honoured and so nourishing, is now a bitter taste, sometimes positively nauseating.'
60 The magazine said the authorities were ramming Gaelic down throats, rather than coaxing it; another difficulty was that Gaelic in Ireland – as in Scotland – was associated with defeat, starvation and impotence.

In 1963 a prominent Irish sociologist, E.F. O'Doherty, predicted:
65 'The fear that we may be lost as a cultural or political entity in the world of the future is only too well grounded if our thinking is that we must resist or resent change and merely preserve the past.'

The call for change carried echoes of the Scottish poet Hugh
70 MacDiarmid, who sought a 'Gaelic Idea' that would be a modern answer to 'the quasi-genocidal destruction of Gaelic culture in Scotland'. In Ireland, Wales and Scotland, language enthusiasts believe the Idea has arrived. Even in Brittany, where Celtic expression had been given short shrift by successive
75 governments, 'positive' remarks by President Chirac have prompted Breton-speakers to campaign for their own Breton television.

How has this transformation come about? At the Galway headquarters of Teilifis na Gaeilge, director Cathal Goan, a
80 bearded Belfast man from the Ardoyne, acknowledges the European paradox: that, far from submerging minority languages, Europe is saving them. 'More and more are travelling and working abroad, especially within the European Union,' he says. 'You often hear Irish people saying they are taken to be
85 English because they speak English. They may not enjoy that so they want to learn a few words of Irish.'

To be Irish in Europe is to be 'accepted'. Ireland has reaped great benefit from European membership and is regarded as a staunchly European country. Her music is highly popular, her
90 poets win Nobel prizes and her writers Booker prizes, Irish theatre, Irish 'pop', Irish-based *Riverdance* are all part of the 'Gaelic Idea'. Because Britain's reluctance to Europeanise herself is widely perceived as English intransigence, the Celtic regions do not mind distancing themselves from that perception.
95 In Dublin's redeveloped Temple Bar, on the South bank of the Liffey, Tom Sherlock, a musicologist with Cladagh Records, says the Gaelic resurgence is 'a reflection of the cultural vibrancy in the country. With the country doing well economically, the young people are more self-confident.'

◄ What may be the reasons Ireland made Irish its first language?

to editorialise to express an opinion (as a journalist)
solitary only
remnant left-over
to toll to ring slowly and repeatedly
dismally sadly
nauseating ['nɔ:sɪeɪtɪŋ] sickening

to ram s.th. down your throat (inf.) to make you fully understand
to coax to persuade in a gentle way

entity s.th. complete, individual

genocide murder of a whole race or community

to give s.o. /s. th. short shrift to pay very little attention to

to submerge *untergehen*

staunchly very loyally
Booker McConnell Prize annual award given to the best English novel
reluctance unwillingness
intransigence [ɪn'trænsɪdʒəns] refusal to change your attitude
to redevelop *sanieren*

vibrancy vitality

backlash revolt

to dub to synchronize

exchequer (BrE)
Finanzministerium

stronghold bastion

despairing unhappy

Might Ireland be a model for ➤
Europe?
essence soul

In the Dublin offices of Teilifis na Gaeilge, the head of devel- 100
opment and information, Padhraic O Ciardha, believes the station's success will be due partly to a backlash against the material coming out of America and Australia. 'We will not make the
mistake of rebroadcasting dubbed Hollywood,' he says. 'Everything we do here, whether home-grown or editing a Welsh dra- 105
ma, creates jobs.'

Teilifis na Gaeilge receives £10 million a year from the Irish
exchequer, compared with the £70m S4C gets from the Welsh
Office and the £8.6m government contributions to the Scottish
Comataidh Telebhisein Gaidhlig. About one million Irish 110
people (north and south) have some knowledge of Gaelic, half
of them fluent or aiming to be so, but only 70,000 converse daily in it. Gaelic classes are even being conducted on Belfast's
Shankill Road, stronghold of Protestant loyalism.

In 1979 Seamus Deane, the Derry author and one of this 115
year's Booker prize nominees, reflected: 'Nothing is more mo-
notonous or despairing than the search for the essence which
defines a nation.' Seventeen years on, the Celtic nations believe
they have it. Jones says: 'The essence of Europe is its diversity.
In these islands at the moment we are seeing how it is possible 120
to have diverse cultures and to coexist.'

Activities

Drawing a diagram ➤

Work together with a partner. Read the text again paragraph
by paragraph and draw a diagram to display the contents of
the text. You may start in the following way:

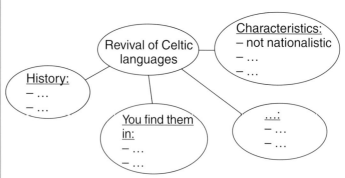

Use an overhead transparency and present your results to
the whole class for discussion.

The importance of ➤
Gaelic

In groups, find arguments from the text why Gaelic, a language spoken only by a tiny minority, is so important for people.
Present the arguments in class and discuss whether you can
agree with them.

Chapter 5: "A sense of what a dialogue among Neanderthals might have been like" – Language and Modern Media

Start here

Discussion ➤ To critics, modern media such as TV, radio, or the computer have many disadvantages:

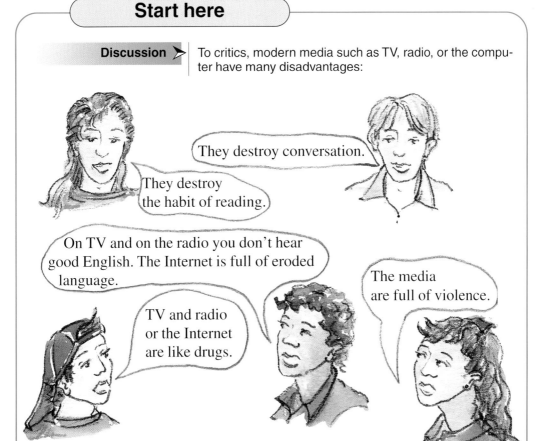

They destroy conversation.

They destroy the habit of reading.

On TV and on the radio you don't hear good English. The Internet is full of eroded language.

TV and radio or the Internet are like drugs.

The media are full of violence.

In groups or in class, discuss these statements. Can you also find arguments for modern media?

Language Threatened

Michael Heim

The following text deals with the computer and what it has done to language.
In class, discuss how the computer has changed your lives.

The computer ➤

manic behaving in a very anxious and excited way

What is meant by "tidal wave ➤ of written words"?

literacy the ability to read and write

Observe the author's attitude ⋎ towards word-processed manuscripts.

submission here: *Beiträge*

prolix using more words than necessary

bloated swollen

profuse very large

garbled *durcheinander*

reams very large amount of s.th.

What do you learn about the ⋎ history of word processing?

lure *Verlockung*

to hook *ködern*

retrieval getting information back

to streamline to make more effective

quantum leap *Quantensprung*

mainframe large computer

number crunching (inf.) *Zahlenverarbeitung*

What is the state of the language? No state at all. It is in process. Our language is being word-processed. If languages have states of health, get sick or well, then ours is manic.

We face a tidal wave of written words. The wave of future shock swelled on the horizon. First came speed reading – a 5 twentieth-century version of literacy. Next Xerox duplication, the word processor, and the fax machine. Now we drive a technology that drives our verbal life faster and faster. The word processor is computerizing our language.

Word-processed submissions have doubled the workload of 10 editors at commercial and academic presses. Writers grow prolix, with manuscripts bloated to twice normal size. The prose is profuse, garbled, torturously disorganized – as if the difference between writing and revising were passé. Pages are becoming more difficult to read. Reams of paper pour out unedited 15 streams of consciousness. The only writer who admits he is no faster than he was before computers is Isaac Asimov, who published 141 books in 138 months.

Before 1980 the microcomputer was a crude, costly kit for hobbyists and experimenters. Then Dan Bricklin and Dan Fyl- 20 stra created software for an electronic spreadsheet (an accounting tool for figuring finances in rows and columns). *Visicalc* ran on the Apple II and opened the market for desktop computers. In 1981 International Business Machines (IBM) persuaded business that computerized spreadsheets would increase pro- 25 ductivity. Once installed, computers could also run other software including word processing. The lure of greater productivity hooked professional writers too. By now most writers use word processing.

IBM first coined the term *word processing* in 1964 to de- 30 scribe a brand of typewriter. The MTST (Magnetic Tape "Selectric" Typewriter) boasted word-processing capabilities because it used magnetic tape to store pages of text. You could select pages for retrieval from electronic memory, which greatly streamlined the production of texts. Machines dedicated solely 35 to word-processing, like the Wang, soon appeared. The quantum leap in writing technology, however, came with microcomputers. The broad base of micro users allowed word-processing software to flourish. A decade earlier, data processors had used text-editing software on mainframe computers to create pro- 40 grams for number crunching. Their editing programs applied information-processing techniques rather than allow direct human interaction with texts on video monitors. When video arrived, inventors like Doug Engelbart und Ted Nelson saw the computers could do more than aid mechanical typewriting. 45

They believed word processing could amplify mental powers and increase our command over language. Word processing ceased being a typing gadget and became a cultural phenomenon. Over 80 percent of computer use is now word processing.
50 Today computers spew out the major bulk of written English.

During the 1980s a new vocabulary established the computerization of English. To be initiated, you had to repeat buzzwords like *access, input,* and *output.* You learned to speak of *files* having no apparent physical dimensions, *menus* offering a
55 selection of nonedibles, and *monitors* providing vigilance over your own words. You learned to navigate with *wraparound* and with a *cursor* – sometimes dubbed *cursee* as it became the recipient of your profanities. You may have even explored *mouse compatibility,* the *ASCII* code, and the difference be-
60 tween *RAM* and *ROM* memory. At the very least, you addressed yourself to *floppies* and *windows,* to *function keys* and program *documentation* (read: instruction manual). You had to take into account *block moves, hyphenation zones,* and *soft spaces* versus *hard.* The editorial *cut-and-paste* became yours electronically.
65 You learned not only to *delete* but also to *unerase,* then to *search-and-replace,* and onward to *globally search-and-replace. Automatic formatting* and *reformatting* entered your writing routine.

Once initiated into the basics of word processing you sigh,
70 this is bliss! No more cutting paper and pasting, no more anxiety about revisions. Now you can get to work without the nuisance of typing and retyping. Words dance on the screen. Sentences slide smoothly into place, making way for one another, while paragraphs ripple rhythmically. Words become highlight-
75 ed, vanish and then reappear instantly at the push of a button. Digital writing is nearly frictionless. You formulate thoughts directly on screen. You don't have to consider whether you are writing the beginning, middle, or end of your text. You can snap any passage into any place with the push of a key. The flow of
80 ideas flashes directly on screen. No need to ponder or sit on an idea – capture it on the fly!

But the honeymoon fades, and the dark side of computing descends upon you. The romance with computers shows its pathological aspects: mindless productivity and increased
85 stress.

Your prose now reads, well, differently. You no longer formulate thoughts carefully before beginning to write. You think on screen. You edit more aggressively as you write, making changes without penalty of retyping. Possible changes occur to
90 you rapidly and frequently, so that a leaning tower of printouts stretches from the wastebasket to the heights of perfection – almost. The power at your fingertips tempts you to believe that faster is better, that ease means instant quality.

---

to amplify to increase power

gadget small useful machine

to spew out *ausspeien, auswerfen*

buzzword *Modewort*

◄ How would you translate these words into German?

vigilance watchfulness

recipient *Empfänger*

cutting and pasting the activity of moving words from one place to another on a computer screen

to initiate into to teach s.o. about
◄ Is this the author's real opinion?
bliss happiness

to ponder to think about s.th. carefully

to descend upon s.b. *über jmd. hereinbrechen*

leaning tower *schiefer Turm*

Activities

Your reaction to the text

Do you agree with Michael Heim's arguments? First, use the following scale to record your measure of agreement:

1	2	3	4	5

Do not agree
at all

I'm very much of
the same opinion

Second, find other students with the same score. Discuss your reasons for awarding this score. Third, together find students with scores very different from yours. Try to convince them.
In class, talk about reasons why your reactions could have been so different.

Advantages and disadvantages of the computer

Work together in groups. Make a list of works and daily routines you have to do for school. Then discuss advantages and disadvantages of using a computer to help you complete your tasks.
One of you should take notes during your discussion and report your findings back to the whole class.

The rhetorical structure of the text

Michael Heim uses certain figures of speech in his text:

- **alliteration** (the use of words which begin with the same consonants)
- **anaphora** (repetition of a word or phrase at the beginning of successive sentences or paragraphs)
- **climax** (expressions arranged in such a way that they become more impressive and effective)
- **irony** (the use of words that are the opposite of what you really mean)
- **metaphor** (a comparison that cannot be taken literally, such as "the sunshine of her smile" or "the city is a jungle")
- **personification** (things and objects are presented as if they were alive)
- **rhetorical question** (a question asked without expecting an answer)

> **Figurative or metaphorical language** is a deviation of standard language to achieve some special meaning or effect.

In pairs, find examples of these in the text and present them to your class. Then discuss why the author might use figurative language.

Bards of the Internet

Philip Elmer-Dewitt

Before you read the following text talk about what you know already about the Internet, Cyberspace, or E-mail.

◁ **Talking about the Internet**

One of the unintended side effects of the invention of the telephone was that in many countries writing went out of style. Oh, sure, there were still full-time scribblers – journalists, academics, professional wordsmiths. And the great centers of com-
5 merce still found it useful to keep on hand people who could draft a memo, a brief, a press release or a contract. But given a choice between picking up a pen or a phone, many folks took the easy route and gave their fingers – and sometimes their mind – a rest.

◁ Think about the pros and cons of writing a letter vs. using the phone.
CompuServe, Prodigy, America Online Commercial online services with a large choice of activities and usually a gateway to the Internet

10 Which makes what's happening on the computer networks all the more startling. Every night in the U.S., for example, when they should be watching television, millions of computer users sit down at their keyboards; dial into CompuServe, Prodigy, America Online or the Internet; and start typing – electronic
15 mail, bulletin-board postings, chat messages, rants, diatribes, even short stories and poems. Just when the media of MacLuhan were supposed to render obsolete the medium of Shakespeare, the online world is experiencing the greatest boom in letter writing since the 18th century.

◁ For a bulletin-board posting see box
rants foolish things said to show disapproval
diatribe extremely critical article, attack
to render to make to become
overwhelming überwältigend

20 "It is my overwhelming belief that E-mail and computer conferencing is teaching an entire generation about the flexibility and utility of prose," writes Jon Carroll, a columnist at the San Francisco *Chronicle*. Patrick Nielsen Hayden, an editor at Tor Books in New York City, compares electronic bulletin boards
25 with the "scribblers' compacts" of the late 18th and early 19th centuries, in which members passed letters from hand to hand, adding a little more at each turn. David Sewell, an associate editor at the University of Arizona, likens netwriting to the literary scene Mark Twain discovered in San Francisco in the 1860s,
30 "when people were reinventing journalism by grafting it onto the tall-tale folk tradition". Others hark back to the American Revolutionary War pamphleteers, or even to the Elizabethan era, when, thanks to Gutenberg, a generation of English writers became intoxicated with language.

to graft onto aufpfropfen, übertragen
to hark back to remember or to remind s.o. of s.th.
intoxicated to behave in a wild and excited way
∀ Compare the views you have just read about with the following objections.

35 But such comparisons invite a question: If online writing today represents some sort of renaissance, why is so much of it so awful? For it can be very bad indeed: sloppy, meandering, puerile, ungrammatical, poorly spelled, badly structured and at times virtually content free. "HEY!!!1!" reads an all too typical
40 message on the Internet, "I THINK METALLICA IZ REEL KOOL DOOD!1!!!"

sloppy messy, careless, muddled
meandering [mɪ'ændərɪŋ] not having a structure
puerile ['pjʊərɑɪl] silly, childish

One reason, of course, is that E-mail is not like ordinary writing. "You need to think of this as 'written speech'," says Gerard Van der Leun, a Connecticut literary agent who has emerged as
45 one of the pre-eminent stylists on the Net. "These things are little more considered than coffee-house talk and a lot less con-

pre-eminent outstanding

sidered than a letter. They're not to have and hold; they're to fire and forget." Many online postings are composed "live" with the clock ticking, using rudimentary word processors on computer systems that charge by the minute and in some cases will shut 50 down without warning when an hour runs out.

That is not to say that with more time every writer on the Internet would produce sparkling copy. Much of the fiction and poetry is second-rate or worse, which is not surprising given 55 that the barriers to entry are so low. "In the real world," says Mary Anne Mohanraj, a Chicago-based poet, "it takes a hell of a lot of work to get published, which naturally weeds out a lot of the garbage. On the Net, just a few keystrokes sends your writing out to thousands of readers." 60

ream a large amount

But even among the reams of bad poetry, gems are to be found. Mike Godwin, a Washington-based lawyer who posts under the pen name "mnemonic," tells the story of Joe Green, a technical writer at Cray Research who turned a moribund discussion group called rec.arts.poems into a real poetry workshop 65 by mercilessly critiquing the pieces he found there. "Some people got angry and said if he was such a god of poetry, why didn't he publish his poems to the group?" recalls Godwin. "He did, and blew them all away." Green's *Well Met in Minnesota,* a mock-epic account of a face-to-face meeting with a fellow net- 70 work scribbler, is now revered on the Internet as a classic. It begins, "The truth is that when I met Mark I was dressed as the *Canterbury Tales.* Rather difficult to do as you might suspect, but I wanted to make a certain impression."

What positive examples of ❦ netwriting are mentioned in the following?

gem s.th. especially good
moribund ['mɒrɪbʌnd] s.th. about to come to an end

mock imitation
to revere [rɪˈvɪə] to admire

The more prosaic technical and political discussion groups, 75 meanwhile, have become so crowded with writers crying for attention that a Darwinian survival principle has started to prevail. "It's so competitive that you have to work on your style if you want to make any impact," says Jorn Barger, a software designer in Chicago. Good writing on the Net tends to be clear, 80 vigorous, witty and above all brief. "The medium favors the terse," says Crawford Kilian, a writing teacher at Capilano College in Vancouver, British Columbia. "Short paragraphs, bulleted lists and oneliners are the units of thought here."

85 Some of the most successful netwriting is produced in computer conferences, where writers compose in a kind of collaborative heat, knocking ideas against one another until they spark. Perhaps the best examples of this are found on the WELL, a Sausalito, California, bulletin board favored by journalists. The 90 caliber of discussion is often so high that several publications – including the New York *Times* and the *Wall Street Journal* – have printed excerpts from the WELL.

vigorous s.th. done with a lot of energy
terse *kurz und bündig*

Example of a bulletin-board posting

```
Empfaenger  :   /K12/CHAT/SENIOR
Absender    :   STEVEN3%HOTMAIL.COM@ODS
Betreff     :   Punishment choice, please help
Datum       :   Sa 26.10.96, 20:05 (erhalten: 31.10.96)
Groesse     :   1286 Bytes
-----------------------------------------------------------------------------
Message-ID: <846356372.17477@dejanews.com>
Date: 26 Oct 1996 19:05:57 GMT
Organization: Deja News Usenet Posting Service
X-Gateway: OS osgo.KS.HE.Schule.de [Uranus-Soft Rfc2Art v1.4)

Hi, I need some advice.
I am 13 years old and got into some trouble.
I signed my mom's name to a bad grade that I got in one of my classes.
My parents found out and weren't too happy.
They gave me this choice for punishment.
1. I get grounded for 2 months, this means no TV, Internet, or friends.
OR
2. I get spanked by my dad, then by my mom, on different days.

I found it strange that they would offer the second choice being that I have
never been spanked before, and I am a teen.
I don't want to be grounded, but I also don't want to be spanked like a lit-
tle kid.
They aren't telling me how they will spank me, but they did say that my pants
and boxers would come off!!
I am too old for this, and I am not looking forward to bearing all, espe-
cially in front of my mom!!!

Any suggestions, what punishment would you take?
I have to decide by Wednesday.


-----------------------------------------------------------------------------
This article was posted to Usenet via the Posting Service at Deja News:
http://www.dejanews.com/ [Search, Post, and Read Usenet News!]
```

Activities

Thinking about the article ➤ In pairs, try to give each paragraph of Elmer-Dewitt's article a headline and draw a diagram like the following on an over-head-transparency or on a poster:

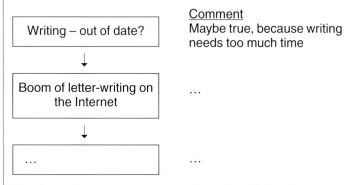

Comment
Maybe true, because writing needs too much time

...

...

For discussion, present your results to the whole class.

Making a comparison ➤ In class, contrast Michael Heim's view on the computer with what is said in Philip Elmer-Dewitt's article.

Talking about E-mail ➤ In class, discuss the pros and cons of E-mail. Also take the arguments of the text into account.

The rich and the poor ➤ Those who can use a computer seem to earn about 15% more than others. In groups, discuss the implications of this fact. Does the computer create a new "apartheid" between rich and poor?
Then write an essay in which you discuss this problem (cf. information box, p. 23) After you have finished, share your essay with another group and discuss your ideas with them.

Acknowledgements

Illustrations

p. 5: Dunlop; p. 7: Pfeiffer – Anthony, Burbeck – Anthony, Traurig – Anthony; p. 14: © AKG, Berlin; p. 17: © Rook/laenderpress; p. 19: © Hanak/laenderpress; p. 24: Burbeck – Anthony; p. 27: © Camera Press/INTERFOTO, Foto: Tom Blau; p. 32: David Cook: Second Best. London: Faber and Faber 1994; p. 36: From WORD WORKS by Cathryn Berger Kaye. Copyright © 1985 by the Yolla Bolly Press. By permission of Little, Brown and Company; p. 42 and p. 46: © AKG, Berlin; p. 50: © Damm/laenderpress; p. 58: © dpa/Carsten Rehder

Texts

Larry E. Smith: "A Chauvinistic Language" from *Readings in English as an International Language,* ed. by Larry E. Smith, Pergamon Press Ltd., Oxford, 1983, pp. 7–9

Loreto Todd: "Pidgins and Creoles" from *Pidgins and Creoles* by Loreto Todd, Routledge, London, 2nd ed. 1990, pp. 1–3

John Agard: "Mek Four" from *The Arnold Anthology of Post-Colonial Literatures in English,* ed. by John Thieme, Arnold, London, 1996

William Shakespeare: "The Red Plague Rid You for Learning Me Your Language" from *The Tempest* by William Shakespeare, ed. by Frank Kermode, Routledge, London, 6th ed. 1958, pp. 30–33

Raja Rao: "Kanthapura" from *The Arnold Anthology of Post-Colonial Literatures in English,* ed. by John Thieme, Arnold, London, 1996, pp. 696–697 and 700

Kim Campbell: "American English – Colonial Substandard or Prestige World Language?" from *The Christian Science Monitor,* 6–12 September 1996, p. 10–11 [original title: "The World Rushes to Speak and Write 'American' English"]. Kim Campbell, *The Christian Science Monitor* © 1997 The Christian Science Publishing Society. All rights reserved. Reprinted with permission.

Stephan Gramley, Kurt-Michael Pätzold: "Spoken Discourse" from *A Survey of Modern English* by Stephan Gramley and Kurt-Michael Pätzold, Routledge, London, 1992, pp. 205–206

Harold Pinter: "Are They Nice?" from *Plays: One* by Harold Pinter, Eyre Methuen, London, 1976, pp. 19–21

David Cook: "It Was Called the Bungalow" from *Second Best* by David Cook, Faber and Faber, London, 1991, pp. 39–42

"Women are better at…" from *Focus,* August 1993, p. 47

Suzanne Romaine: "Men versus Women" from *Language in Society: An Introduction to Sociolinguistics* by Suzanne Romaine, Oxford University Press, Oxford, 1994, pp. 106–107

Carol Shields: "Good Morning, Dr Maloney" from *Mary Swann* by Carol Shields, Harper Collins Publishers, London, 1993, pp. 11–12

Joan Swann: "It is Male Speakers Who Talk More" from *Girls, Boys, and Language* by Joan Swann, Blackwell Publishers, Oxford, 1992, pp. 26–28

Trevor A. Harley: "The Origin of Language" from *The Psychology of Language: From Data to Theory,* Erlbaum (UK) Taylor & Francis Publishers, Hove, 1995, pp. 5–6

Geoffrey Chaucer: "Whan that April…" from *The Complete Works of Geoffrey Chaucer,* ed. by F. N. Robinson, Oxford University Press, Oxford, 2nd ed. 1974, p. 17

Geoffrey Chaucer: "Wenn milder Regen…" from *Die Canterbury Tales* by Geoffrey Chaucer, trans. and ed. by Martin Lehnert, Winkler Verlag, München, 1985, p. 29

Robert McCrum, William Cran, Robert MacNeil: "The Spread of RP" from *The Story of English* by Robert McCrum, William Cran, and Robert MacNeil, Faber and Faber, London, 1986, pp. 26–28

Cal McCrystal: "Proud Celts Reverse Tide of History" from *The Observer*, 17 November 1996, p. 22

Michael Heim: "Language Threatened" from *The State of the Language: 1990 Edition,* ed. by Christopher Ricks and Leonard Michaels, Faber and Faber, London, 1990, pp. 300–302

Philip Elmer-Dewitt: "Bards of the Internet" from *Time: The Weekly Newsmagazine,* 4 July 1994, Vol. 144, No. 1, pp. 62–63